In Gratitude to
My Guardian Angel

In Gratitude to My Guardian Angel

Theresa Patnode

also known as

Theresa M. Santmann

iUniverse, Inc.
New York Lincoln Shanghai

In Gratitude to My Guardian Angel

iUniverse books may be ordered through booksellers or by contacting:

iUniverse
2021 Pine Lake Road, Suite 100
Lincoln, NE 68512
www.iuniverse.com
1-800-Authors (1-800-288-4677)

ISBN: 978-0-595-45747-2 (pbk)
ISBN: 978-0-595-70584-9 (cloth)
ISBN: 978-0-595-90050-3 (ebk)

Printed in the United States of America

To Randall Santmann, my grandson, whom I love very much and who has been invaluable in helping me put this book together.

Contents

Acknowledgment

My sincere thanks to Court Little Rose # 1300 Ellenburg, New York, Catholic Daughters of the Americans who graciously have given me permission to incorporate pictures from their book *Ellenburg Yesterday and Today,* and to family members who helped me assemble family pictures.

1

My Guardian Angel ~ Catholic Church ~ Sin

All of us kids know that each one of us has our very own guardian angel. I think that God is the one who decides which one we are going to get. I like talking to my angel because there are a lot of things I can't say to other kids, my mother and father, or any of my brothers and sisters. After all, who can I talk to about being scared or about other things—like not wanting to pray so much or maybe even about having committed a sin when I wasn't in church where God is up there on the altar to talk to?

I think that my guardian angel likes my name—Theresa—because most of the time I feel my angel quite close to me. I don't know if it is a boy or a girl, but I know my angel is floating in a misty white cloud dressed in a flowing, shimmering, white gown. I wonder if my angel is the reason I quite often dream of the heavenly feeling of being able to fly.

In church, if one of us kids sits back with our behind on the wooden church bench when we are supposed to be kneeling up straight, Ma reaches over and gives the kid a poke to kneel up straight no matter how long he or she has been kneeling up straight on the narrow wooden kneeler. Even if she can't reach, a look from her is enough to make a kid kneel up straight in a hurry. Dad doesn't seem to care. I've never seen him give anybody a poke or even a mean look about not kneeling up straight.

Sometimes being in church is super nice, and sometimes it's not very nice at all, especially when the priest keeps talking about all our sins and that we'll end up going to hell if we don't change our sinful ways. Some of the nice times have to do with feeling that God likes me a whole lot and I can talk directly to him. One of those times is during mass when the priest lifts up the white, flat, round Eucharist, which is about three inches across and that is God. Another time is

1

when I have just received Communion by going to the alter rail and having a much smaller Eucharist put on my tongue by the priest.

All that talk about the body and blood of Christ, with the little piece of bread being his body and the wine in the chalice being his blood, doesn't seem to make too much sense. When I can think about being closer to God by going to receive Holy Communion so that I can talk directly to him, it makes me feel better—especially if my mother or one of the other kids has called me a bad girl. My father never calls me bad. The priests keep talking about the devil and how he is always coaxing everybody to do bad things. That sure makes it awfully hard not to do something that is a sin. I guess the only way I can keep from being bad is to be very careful about everything that the devil might try to get me to do.

There are all kinds of things that are sins: bad thoughts and bad deeds like lying or stealing or fighting, or using God's name in vain. There seem to be sins in all kinds of things that people do. I think pride is one of the hardest sins not to be guilty of. Is it really bad to want to look pretty? The two teeth that should have come in between my eyeteeth and my two front teeth after my baby teeth fell out never grew in, so I sure don't smile very much. I sometimes look in a mirror and try to see how I can smile without showing that they are missing. When I feel happy, I try to smile like I practiced in front of the mirror so the gaps don't show very much. It is pretty darn hard.

There are beautiful stained-glass windows full of pictures about God and saints in our church—St. Edmund's, in Ellenburg Corners, New York. When the sun comes through the tall, narrow windows, the colors come out like the vivid colors in our neighbor Mrs. Smith's flower garden. The reds are like the shimmering color of a dew-covered red rose, the blue is like the colors of a morning glory pointing toward the blue sky, and the green is like that of newly sprouted spring grass. I love them so.

The one window that all us kids and my dad, and I think even my mother, are very proud of is a window near our very own church pew, which is four rows from the front on the right side facing the altar. Our pew is on the left side of the aisle. On our right is the very special family window. My father's family must have paid a lot of money to have their name on the window. There it is at the bottom of the window with the words "Given in honor of the Virgin Mary." On the right side the wording reads "by Mr. and Mrs. Peter Patenaude and Family." Mr. and Mrs. Patenaude are my very own grandmother and grandfather. The rest of the family includes my aunts and uncles, and, of course, my father.

The window shows the Virgin Mary standing in front of a wine-colored heavy drape hung on a rod over which is a field of green grass and trees and a brilliant blue sky. She is wearing a white head scarf that is surrounded by a halo. Her arms are outstretched from a flowing red garment with the palms of her hands set in a beseeching manner facing outward. Over the red garment is an intense blue shoulder wrap that is draped at her waist and then flows on to the floor. Her heart is shown over her clothing as a gesture of her love. The toes of her left foot peek out from under her flowing red dress.

On the walls, about four feet from the floor on both sides of the church, hang the fourteen stations of the cross, which are somewhere between a picture and a statue. The carved figures stick out about an inch. The stations are made of a material that looks like gray clay. They are about two feet high and one and one-half feet wide. The stations are hung in order and tell the story of the crucifixion from the beginning to end. Mostly big people, and kids when mothers and fathers make them, "make" the stations of the cross. That means I start thinking and praying at the first station where Jesus starts to make the trip to his hanging on the cross, all the way to his coming alive again at the last station.

Why do a lot of big people use the word "bad" so much? Our teacher, Miss Carpenter, doesn't use that word. She might raise her voice, but she never uses that awful word. After all, the word "bad" is very closely connected to hell and the devil. I sure hear the word "bad" an awful lot of times from Ma, and the word "hell" from the priest on the altar. They both make sure we know that our chances of getting at least to purgatory, if not to heaven, are going to be a lot better if we do what they tell us to do, like say all the many prayers every day, go to mass at least once a week, go to confession at least once a month, and do the stations of the cross at least at Easter time.

I'd probably have a better chance of not ending up in hell if I tried not to think about things like hating the awfully long prayers or the awfully long sermons where the priest tells us how bad we are and how close we are to eternal damnation if we do or don't do certain things.

That word "eternal"—we all sure know about it's meaning, which is to burn in hell forever in the next world. No wonder my mother and father work so hard to keep us from eternal damnation. What makes me feel better about things like that is when I talk directly to God. He knows that I am really a good girl. I just know in my heart that, no matter what anybody does or does not say, God knows the truth about me. I sure wish that sometimes somebody would actually say something special like, "I like you." That would make me so happy. Actually, my fifty-one-week-older sister Rose comes as close as anybody to letting me know she likes me when she says nice things about my horseback riding, my sewing, my made-up songs, and things like that.

My first memory of St. Edmund's Church is my father carrying me down the aisle on his shoulder, so I must have been about two. I felt so proud, even as such a little kid. My big, strong daddy was carrying me way up there in front of all the people in church. As more and more kids were born into our family, our line at the Communion rail on Sunday kept getting longer and longer, until we finally ended up with Ma and Dad and twelve kids!

It seems so easy for some people to say mean things about the large number of kids in my family. I feel very bad about that. There is only one other family in all the three Ellenburgs that has as many kids. Their house is on the main road between Ellenburg Center and Ellenburg Corner. I don't think the house is part of a farm because I don't see a barn near the house. It seems to me they probably get some kind of government help.

It is so hard to try and stay proud when all the city kids have only two or three kids in their families and the farm kids almost always have so many more. I think that makes most of the city kids stuck up because, for one thing, they have much nicer clothes than farm kids. Almost all our clothes except underwear are hand-me-downs from the older kids in our family, or they come out of the big boxes of clothes that my Aunt Clarinda sends us that she gets from her rich Buffalo, New York, Catholic Church people.

One of the things about being in church is that sometimes it isn't as lonely as being at home with my very noisy brothers and sisters where there isn't anybody I can talk to. I am so sad when my mother is unhappy and talks loud, which seems to happen more often as the family grows and we keep getting poorer. The church is where it is quiet—well, at least the kind of quiet where nobody talks except the priest saying mass or the people singing in the choir.

Besides that, I can talk directly to God even when I'm not receiving Communion. After all, there he is right up there in the tabernacle, which is his little house on the altar. He is inside in the form of consecrated bread called the Eucharist in a gold cup called a chalice. I know words like "chalice" and "tabernacle" and "Eucharist" because my mother and father know those words and they are used a lot in the Catholic Church.

I don't know what I would do without my guardian angel at my house. No matter how sad something makes me or how bad a dream I have, at least my angel isn't far away. After all, that's what angels are for—to watch over you.

2

One-Room Schoolhouse ~ Milk Strike

The bookcase in our one-room schoolhouse is so very important to me. I think that I like it more than any of the other kids. It sits on the back wall of the classroom next to the door that goes to a little hall with a door to outside. The bookcase is a rather clumsy affair, about six feet high and six feet across. Its front and sides are made of skinny little strips of varnished wood with a little wooden line running between the strips. The two hinged doors open from the center. The top has about three inches of graduated overhang. I treasure it so. I have looked at, if not read, every single book it holds.

There is one that I particularly like that somehow never made it back to the bookcase—*Thad and the G-Man*. I wonder if that will count against me in the next world as a venial sin. I don't think it will be a mortal sin. Well, it sure is too late to bring it back because I've had it for about a year and I still haven't been caught. I wonder what Miss Carpenter would say if somehow she found out from one of my tattletale sisters who looked inside the book's cover and saw that it hadn't been returned by the date on the card.

The very best thing about our school is the traveling library. Every month, twenty-five to thirty books come in a cardboard box, and we send back the box of books from the month before. I never miss one—not even one. But, boy, do I have to be a sneak. At night in my house—probably it is to save money—there is only a ten-watt bulb left on in the upstairs hall. It's hard to read when I can barely make out the words. We are supposed to be sleeping, not reading in bed. No wonder I've been wearing glasses since the fourth grade! Mostly it's those darn big boys who see my glasses as a chance to make fun of another kid; but it does make me just a very little bit special—even though the glasses have metal rims. After all, there aren't any other kids with glasses. Some of the teasing comes from big boys like Clarence and Ross, which isn't so bad. I kind of like boys, and at least then they are looking at me.

Our one-room schoolhouse has no running water, so almost every day two of us kids have to go to one of the two closest houses—our house a quarter mile south or the Dominic house a quarter mile north—to get a pail of water. When we get back, one of us pours the water into a tan-colored, ceramic, barrel-shaped water jug, which is about one and one-half feet high with its fat little belly about three feet around. A little faucet in the front is where the water comes out.

The jug sits on a little shelf next to the bookcase. On the shelf and to the left of the jug is a speckled, dark blue enameled washbasin. We can't wash our hands very much because most of the water is needed for drinking. The soap for hand washing comes from a round, two-cup glass holder suspended on the wall over the washbasin. When we push up on a little metal button on the bottom, liquid soap comes out. Little waxed-paper drinking cups can be clicked out of a skinny, round, eighteen-inch-high glass cup holder that is attached to the wall next to the soap dish. The bucket we use to collect the water from the farmhouses is kept under the shelf.

Getting the water bucket filled has its very own set of problems. There seems to be a mostly quiet little war going on between our Protestant teacher Miss Carpenter and my mother. My mother makes sure that we always get water by twos to keep us guarded from evil. I haven't figured out what kind of evil might lurk if one of us goes alone. Of course, there are Protestants as well as Catholics everywhere. Who can tell? The Protestants might somehow steer us away from our Catholic faith. Then there are so many Catholics who don't go to church every Sunday, or maybe they go only on days like Easter and Christmas. I think some of them probably never saw the inside of a confessional—or they may actually be "fallen-away" Catholics. What if some kid like that gave us bad ideas? Actually, I don't know what religion some of the kids are because I don't see them in church and religion is not something any of us talks about.

Miss Carpenter sure knows better than to have one boy and one girl get water. That sure would be asking for trouble. I'm sure she knows she would hear from my mother about that. Kids from our family never visit or play at other kids' houses, and other kids never visit or play at our house. There isn't much time anyway for visiting or playing, except for recess at school. One of the things I love about recess is seeing how high I can make a swing go. It does get a little scary when I get it to go so high that, all the way at the top, the swing chain clanks and hangs loose for a couple of seconds way up there in the air.

Miss Carpenter tries to be fair, but that darn Antoinette is such a sneak. She describes, in the sweetest tones, tasty things they are having at her house for lunch. Miss Carpenter always answers Antoinette just as sweetly about those darn good lunches she is always being invited to. I think Miss Carpenter did try to divide the treasured water trips evenly between the two closest houses—Antoinette's and ours. In fact, I think there probably are more trips to our house because of my mother. When we go for water, Antoinette's mother never complains about the possibility of her kid staying too long at our house. Her mother doesn't seem to care if there might be some kind of sinful mischief that we kids might be up to, but my mother knows better. Antoinette's family almost never goes to church, and I think that Protestant Miss Carpenter likes Antoinette's parents better than mine just because they never complain about anything.

All we Patnode kids go home for lunch. I always try to help my mother with the younger kids during lunchtime. After all, I'm ten years old. There are always diapers to change and, of course, the little kids have to eat too. I sure wish my mother sometimes said nice things to me. There doesn't seem to ever be any time when nice things are said by anybody to another person.

When I am sad, there are things on the earth and in the sky that help me. It can be a small stream splashing over rocks while speckled little fish dart about in cool sparkling clear water, brown soil with its special earthy smell when it's freshly turned, blackberries and raspberries so sweet when eaten straight from the bushes, the intense smell of freshly cut hay, the tiny buds of spring flowers, and green grass peeking out of the recently frozen earth, the cows bellowing out in joy upon their spring release, the wild purple lilies in back of the barn along the little stream fed by water from the well, the first chorus of grasshoppers, wiggly pollywogs in the puddles of marshy earth made squashy from the spring thaw and, of course, at last, the sun that has finally reached through those wintry blasts to melt the snow and warm not only the air, but the frozen earth and us kids.

The warm sun is so wonderfully freeing. Finally, I can stop trying to stay warm by bundling as best I can (and still feel so very cold). Even when we are lucky enough to get them, the cheapest Sears Roebuck or Montgomery Ward catalog snowsuits are not made to keep out the howling winds that come from the frigid north. Even if my mother is going to buy a few snowsuits, I feel pretty sure that Rose, Rita, or almost any other kid will get one before I do. I sure wish my mother liked me more.

In the winter, when the temperature outside gets to be near zero, our school sure is freezing before a fire gets going in the stove. Clarence is a big sixth grader who lives on a farm about a quarter of a mile north of our schoolhouse. He is paid five dollars a month to get up early each school day, go down to our one-room schoolhouse, and build a fire in the potbellied stove. He gets busy with chores and often gets to school only a half hour before we do. For that much money, I would build a fire at least a couple of hours before school starts, but they don't give girls the job of janitor. I don't know why. I would do a much better job then Clarence. When Clarence is late building a fire, we can see our breath anywhere in the room but near the stove. The cold is a good excuse for frequent poking of the fire in our potbellied stove. Any hot coals that fall out of the stove are caught by a square, beat-up tin sheet under it that keeps the floor from catching fire. It is an old, wooden floor, and quite black from semiyearly oiling.

Miss Carpenter sure has no trouble with us asking to go to what is ashamedly referred to as the "basement" even though there is no basement. Our toilet rooms consist of boy and girl two-seaters, one on each end of the small, enclosed entranceway where there is no heat. When we go into the girls' two-seater, we always make sure to use the hook that serves as a lock. It would be just like those darn boys to peek in when we had our pants down whenever they got a chance and they didn't think that Miss Carpenter would catch them. Would that give them something to laugh about, and, of course, Miss Carpenter wouldn't know why they were laughing. Oh yeah, the farm boys sure know how to make fun if they catch a glimpse high up our legs when we are on the swings.

The entrance door to the school is a wooden affair that is really quite wonderful. There are long, skinny cracks in it that provide peepholes for us kids. After I'd been going to school for a couple of years, Miss Carpenter got a boyfriend and we found out about him. She would excuse herself from the classroom and say she'd be back in a minute, but we knew better. She and her boyfriend probably had already arranged a time to meet in front of the school. One of the older boys, who wasn't as scared as the rest of us, would go and peek through the outside door. There she would be in the car smooching. She was never gone very long, but once we found out, most of us kids rushed to the door with the big boys higher up and us littler kids farther down, all peeking out at Miss Carpenter. There sure was scrambling back to our seats when she started getting out of the car.

Back to lunchtime. I think Miss Carpenter did actually go to Antoinette's house a couple of times. It probably was when Antoinette had bragged up something really tasty, like tuna fish in a flour-thickened butter and milk sauce over mashed potatoes or white bread. Even the bread was special. From what Antoinette says, they have store-bought bread, while ours is homemade. All of us kids sure know that store-bought stuff is better than homemade, no matter what it is.

I'm not sure how we know that, we just do. Sometimes for lunch, if Ma has been too busy with the little kids or whatever, crackers, bread, or cereal with milk and sugar is lunch.

Our lunch, if my mother has been able to get around to it, probably is home-made vegetable soup and homemade white bread with awful-tasting margarine. A little yellow coloring packet comes with the white, lardy-looking margarine. Sometimes Ma drops the contents of the packet onto the margarine and leaves the margarine on top of the warming closet of the kitchen stove too long. The margarine melts, then hardens again, leaving the coloring from the packet a yucky-looking mess, or it might not be mixed up enough and the yellow-orange streaks through the white margarine look pretty awful. Sometimes, Ma doesn't have time to put the coloring in at all, and it is just too much to put that white stuff on bread.

Of course, we can't afford butter. The butter would have to be made from cream taken off the top of the milk in the milk cans in the barn before they are sent to the Sealtest plant. Farmers don't know when Sealtest is going to take sneaky tests of the milk. The farmers take their milk cans by horse-drawn wagons in summer, and sleds in winter, to the Sealtest finishing plant in Ellenburg Center. Sometimes the Sealtest people stick a little test tube into one of the cans to check for cream content. I don't know if they test for other things too. Farmers are paid by how much cream there is in the milk as well as by the amount of milk. It sure would be awful if the milk tested was from a can that had a lot of cream taken off the top. We use twelve quarts of milk a day for our family. Dad brings the milk to the house in a twelve-quart pail after the morning chores. Often, even twelve quarts isn't enough, and some milk has to be saved from the evening milking for the evening meal.

My father does take little chances. Every morning when he comes in from the chores, not only does he bring the twelve-quart pail of milk, but he also brings a cup brimming with cream that he has ladled off the top of one of the milk cans from the milking done the night before. The cans are left overnight in a water-filled, cement bathtub-like place in the milk house floor. "Them that gets there first gets the most" certainly is the rule. I'm pretty sure that whoever is in the kitchen when my father comes in from the barn with the cup of cream takes a very big share, because that's what I do. Sometimes, if I'm being real bad, I can get almost the whole cup. Being selfish sure is a sin, but cream on cornflakes tastes so good that sometimes a kid might not care very much about the sin part.

One thing that seems very funny to me is what government people sometimes give to poor people. Of course, at first my father was too proud to take government handouts until finally they were just too much to resist. There are too many kids and we are just too poor. The box has large three- or four-pound chunks of real butter, whole wheat flour, which sometimes has a few small wormy-looking bugs in it, and cornmeal. I love the taste of the butter, even if it isn't anywhere near as good as the butter we make ourselves during a milk strike. Some of the other kids probably have their own butter at home, but it sure isn't something anybody talks about.

I think Miss Carpenter knows better than to say anything to us farm kids about any of this. After all, she has never lived on a real farm. Sometimes she tells us about a couple of her chickens or her little garden, but that doesn't really count. Of course, we are curious to know what kind of a house she lives in and what it looks like, but she lives up a little dead-end road a quarter mile north from the state road that goes east and west through Ellenburg Center. What possible excuse could any of us kids have for going up her road when none of us knows anybody else who lives there?

There are just so many things to think about. It seems to me that I am just about the only kid that Miss Carpenter tells to stop daydreaming and get to work. I can look out of the window at the sparkling heavenly shapes of icy lace on the glass in winter or the turning to green of a spring wonderland and think about all kinds of different things. In my thoughts I can be anywhere. I can be alone or with anybody. I can talk to God or my guardian angel about anything, but I sure wish I could make some of my thoughts come true. Maybe I can.

A couple of times, when the money paid by Sealtest for the farmers' milk seemed unfair, some of the farmers got together to decide whether to strike. When there was a strike, my father led the striking farmers. I was proud of my father for being a leader. The littler kids wouldn't know about my father doing that. The things the striking farmers did to the milk tanks on their truck beds at the Sealtest plant in Ellenburg Depot were sure going to be hard to fix once those angry farmers got through with them. My father has a shotgun and a rifle that he keeps on the top shelf in the washroom. I'm sure my father wouldn't kill anyone, but knowing what farmers bring to the strike (like winter tire chains and rifles) and that they would be milling around the Sealtest trucks in Ellenburg Depot, waiting for Dad to come home was awful. If a farmer turned out to be a scab who kept taking his milk to the plant during a strike, he sure had to pay a price. Kerosene in milk cans sure doesn't leave milk that Sealtest wants to buy.

In our barn there is a door that leads into a ten-foot-by-ten-foot part of the northeast corner of the main barn that opens into the milk house. That is the way most of us use to get into the barn. Then we go through another door into a three-foot-square space, then through another door. Then we are among the rows of cows, calves, and our three horses. During a strike, separating the milk to skim milk, and cream sure keeps my father busy when he isn't busy getting the farmers to help him fight the company to try and get more money for their milk.

As you come into the milk house from outdoors, you see, on the far wall, two sections of what look like sunken cement bathtubs that are kept filled with water. The milk cans filled from the evening milking are placed in the cement bathtubs to cool. They are lifted out the next morning for the trip to the Sealtest factory. To the right of the cement tubs is a metal-sheathed sink, eight inches deep and about two feet by three feet on two-and-one-half-foot legs. That's where milk pails are washed and then turned upside down on heavy metal wire shelves on the wall over the cement bathtubs. There is a third door in the milk house that goes to the much older eastern part of the barn that opens into the carriage house. A couple of old beat-up cutters that are small sleighs with one seat pulled by one horse that aren't used anymore are in the far corners. Hens lay eggs under the cracked leather seats.

In the milk house, there is a machine called a separator, which is for separating the cream from the milk during a strike. It is in the corner between the north and west doors. It has a large stainless steel bowl at the top that holds up to twelve quarts of milk. When it's running, a very small stream of cream comes out one way, and the skim milk goes back into one of the milk cans from another place. This is always a sad time. Will we get any more money for milk? How long will this go on? These are scary questions. After all, even a small milk check is better than none at all. Striking is especially sad when people like Mr. and Mrs. Smith, who have always been our only good friends and closest neighbors, are trying to send their milk to the factory. There are nighttime visits to scab farmers, and secret meetings. How very awful. Maybe Mrs. Smith won't like me any more. There are lots of whispers in school. Sometimes it's very hard to tell who is on what side.

During strikes, we make delicious butter from the cream, and our family, plus the calves and pigs, drink as much of the milk as we can. The rest gets dumped into the brook in back of the barn. It's kind of funny to think of that brook running through the striking George Smith pastureland; well, really not funny at all. Whispers and sideways looks just seem to linger on for years after a strike. Now that I think about it, the butter doesn't taste so good after all.

The front of our schoolhouse faces toward the dirt road on the east. The small entrance hall, with its four doors and two windows, is the only way in. The door to the right leads to the boys' two-seater toilet, and the door to the left leads to the girls' two-seater. There is a small window on the far wall about five feet up in each bathroom. Thank goodness our little window is that high up. I think if they had a chance, the boys would peek inside when we are using the potty. Inside our potty area, which everybody calls the basement, are two twelve-inch round holes in a wooden plank on top of what looks like a wooden box. The plank is the same height from the floor as a real toilet. If anybody looked down the holes there would be the sight of numbers one and two and toilet paper. Somehow, I know that underneath is a holding tank. Sometimes, when the weather gets warm, the smell gets pretty bad. I don't really know for sure, but one time I heard that the tanks are cleaned out once a year. I wonder who does that.

Whenever I ask anybody in my family about anything that has to do with boys and girls together the answer is "You'll find out in your later years." Sometimes, I badly want to talk about something private to anybody in my family, but nobody talks about much of anything to other kids if they don't want their question to come back to the whole family for teasing. What big people and other kids call teasing sure can hurt and be quite cruel.

I guess I'll have to wait till I get older to get answers to a lot of questions I have. Of course, it would be much too embarrassing to try and get answers from people like teachers or other relatives. I want to smack my older sister Rita when she gives me that "later years" answer. My mother isn't any help there either. She already calls me boy crazy. Of course, all you have to do is talk to a boy once and a tattletale brother or sister starts very mean nasty teasing in a mocking voice. I never ask my mother about much of anything. Quite often, even though there are so many kids in my family, I feel so very lonely.

3

School ~ Communism ~ Sin ~ Prayers ~ Church

Communism and sin are really the same and can be found everywhere. Especially in the schools is where my mother, and I suspect my father, find that awful communism, which is sure to damn to hell anyone who falls into its clutches. Communism is the work of the devil, and the devil tries to get your soul anyway he can—and he is everywhere. He certainly can be found in some of the things they are trying to teach us in school. How the earth is made is a good example. Of course, good people know that God made everything. He made the earth, the moon, us, animals—everything. And there is Miss Carpenter, our teacher, trying to tell us something else.

My mother and father think that all this foolishness—actually much more than foolishness—probably started with the superintendent of schools. The only name they ever use for him is Dictator Pumpkin. What do I know? One day in school, when I wanted to say something about that big school far away with all the big kids, I said the superintendent's name as Dictator Pumpkin. I'd never heard anything else at home and he wasn't talked about in school. Miss Carpenter looked at me as if she hated me. "Don't you ever, ever say anything like that again!" Her words didn't keep on going, but every one of them hurt me so bad. My mother thought it was very funny when she heard about it. I am such a good girl, and Miss Carpenter had seemed to like me, at least better than some of the other kids, who talked in class, or got in fights punching each other—sometimes for fun and sometimes when they wanted to hurt another kid.

Family prayers in the morning are much shorter than the evening ones, so everybody is supposed to kneel up very straight for all of the morning prayers. My mother sure tries to squeeze in prayers after the scramble of all the kids getting dressed and then eating a breakfast of oatmeal or Maltex and toast, when there is still a minute before the school bus gets to our house. We say the Our

Father and Hail Mary, and a few other prayers, but, thank goodness, there never is time for the rosary except on weekends. The night prayers sure make up for whatever we might have missed in the morning. The big dining room in the middle of the house is the gathering place for the prayers.

On the north wall is a daybed with a thin mattress next to a stairway that leads to the second floor. I remember that daybed from when I was a little two-year-old kid. My mother told me some of the parts I can't remember about having a mastoid operation. The part I remember was the nighttime. A feeble light drifted down the stairs from a ten- or fifteen-watt bulb. It wasn't exactly pain, but my whole body felt so funny—as if I wasn't made of skin and bones like a real body. She said there was oozing coming out of a little hole left in back of my right ear and she could see some white stuff in the hole, so she pulled out what turned out to be a rather long piece of dressing that had been left inside me.

In the middle of the dining room is a large, dark, wooden, rectangular table with rounded corners. The table has a leaf in the middle and always seems to be covered by a pile of papers and clothes. I guess it's no wonder, since the table is often used for folding clean clothes brought in from outdoors. Also, kids sometimes use the table when they are doing homework. In the east side of the room, at the foot of the daybed, is a door that leads to the kitchen. Between the kitchen door and a window is a five-foot-long buffet with drawers. We kneel looking toward the buffet because, on its long, flat surface, there is an eighteen-inch statue of the Sacred Heart, which rests on a daintily crocheted doily with a lighted candle in front of it. Nobody ever has to be coaxed to light the candle. It is fun using big wooden matchsticks.

Sometimes other smaller statues, novena cards, church bulletins, or a magazine like *The Sacred Heart Messenger* cover every square inch of the buffet. On the wall over the buffet hangs a large picture of martyrs working at saving the pagans in Africa. We know that, quite often, instead of being saved, the natives have done terrible things to the missionaries who were trying to save them from eternal damnation. In the picture, the missionaries are tied up in front of a fire, and you know that the next thing that is going to happen is that they are going to die. The least we can do is try very hard to earn money to send missionaries to help them in their mission of saving souls.

One thing we can do is pick up freshly dug potatoes in the fall for five cents a bushel. There sure aren't very many ways to earn money, and we don't have any relatives who give us money like a grandmother or grandfather, so getting five dollars together to give to our parish priest to send to the missionaries in Africa to save a native usually takes years. Sometimes I think I might want to be a nun, but

I never want to be a missionary in Africa. One time I finally got four dollars together to send to Africa, and I got one of my sisters to put in the other dollar to save a native. Of course, the priest saying that we would have a trip straight to heaven for our five-dollar gift to save a native sure made me want to do it for myself too. I wonder what's going to happen after I die, because I didn't contribute the whole five dollars.

There is fun stuff in the beat-up old buffet with its several missing drawer handles. The long top drawer has all kinds of treasures like baby books and a set of silverware. The baby books are especially fun to look at and read—even though the number of words is rather scanty, like how much we weighed when we were born, who is our godmother and godfather, stuff like that. Other things the drawer holds are stubs of milk checks and church bulletins that sometimes have a list of what people give to the church. The lists sure show up a lot of the church's smarty-pants who give almost nothing to the church. Once my mother and father beat out my very-big-deal Uncle Bill by giving more in a church drive than he did. Of course, we aren't supposed to be poking around in the buffet drawers, but every once in a while I sneak into them when there isn't a squealer in the room like my sister Rita. When nobody else is around, not even another kid, which of course doesn't happen very often, I sometimes do some quick looking around in the drawers.

Uncle Bill has two farms, each of which has a farmhouse. One farm is in Ellenburg Center and the other one is in Ellenburg Depot. He lives in a house separate from his farms in the village of Ellenburg Center. In addition to the farms and his house, he owns a general store with another man. My father tried to get to be his partner in the store but, of course, all French Canadians know that you have to make it on your own and be tough, so Uncle Bill would not take my father as a partner. I guess somehow it might have to do with all the bitter cold winters, or maybe it is to show how big and strong men have to be. Well anyway, no wonder Uncle Bill was such a big deal. In addition to everything else, he is president of the school board that includes all the three Ellenburgs. He doesn't have any kids, and sometimes we hear about all the wonderful things he is collecting for the furnishings of his big house in Ellenburg Center that none of us Sam Patnode kids was ever in.

Actually, sometimes we are able to get the best of him when he runs for some kind of government office. Without his knowing, it is almost too good to be true what we can manage to get. Around the village of Ellenburg Center he has people give out pencils with his name on them, and other people give out candies that are chocolate outside with cream and a cherry inside. The cherry sure lasts a long time when I don't chew it right away. Sometimes, if there is more than one person giving out the chocolates, maybe, just maybe, somebody won't see me sneaking over to the person with the other box. It's a good thing Uncle Bill never catches me.

Even though Uncle Bill is part owner of a store that carries all kinds of wonderful candies spread out in a case under glass, he never offers any of us a piece of candy no matter how many times we stand looking at the yummes. When we are with Dad, who is buying flour or sugar or other things at Uncle Bill's store, he never talks to us or gives us any candy. I wonder if that might have something to do with what I sometimes hear Mom and Dad talking about—the store bill getting very big and our always being so short of money. We kids sure try to make up for his stinginess whenever he runs for something, like head of the school board, and he has pencils and chocolates being handed out in his name.

Well, anyway, back to the church donations. One time, right there in the church bulletin, was the name Samuel Patnode listing the four hundred dollars that my family had pledged. It was more than either Uncle Bill or Uncle Ed's pledge. Of course, we couldn't afford that large amount of money, but we did it anyway. We were sure proud about that amount of money and, of course, in addition, proud of what it was going to do for us in the next world. It would be nice if we could give that much all the time.

What is going to happen to Uncle Bill in the next world? He has no kids. Why does he think people get married? Also, he is the school board president of a school that makes kids take off almost all their clothes for yearly health exams, has kids taking nude showers together, lets the boys and girls mingle together all over the place, and distributes books that probably contain some communist teachings of one kind or another. That by itself will probably keep him from going to heaven.

With my mother and father having all us kids and then having to keep track of so many things, it's no wonder they seem so tired as well as cranky and quite angry most of the time. Of course, they have to holler to be heard, and my mother is cooped up in the house being pregnant so much. I think that it all probably makes her unhappy. To get away from all the noise in the house, I try to make sure I am the girl my father wants helping in the barn and fields. Besides, then I get to do things like get the cows on horseback in the forest. I love animals—especially horses. And everything in the forest is so peaceful. Overhead there usually is a cover of powder blue sky with floating white clouds as I experience the sound of animals, rustling leaves, and earthy smells.

The buffet holds treasures like my mother's most cherished sterling silver-plated knives, forks, and spoons carefully wrapped in embroidered white cotton cloth. Each is in its own little space, and knives, forks, and spoons are rolled into three separate cloth holders. Boy, they sure don't come out very often. There is a long rectangular table linen with twelve matching napkins which never comes out of the drawer. In a bottom drawer to the right are the most precious things: tiny, beautiful baby clothes. They look so new, I wonder if they were ever used. I take them out very carefully, but if I hear somebody coming, I stuff them back in the drawer real quick.

Night prayers seem to go on forever. The rosary is first with its Hail Marys, the Our Fathers—on and on. For the entire rosary, we have to kneel up straight on the hardwood maple dining room floor facing the buffet. Every once in a while, the kids in the back sit their behinds on their heels, but, when Ma catches them, they sure have to kneel up straight in a hurry. If a kid is trying to be a cheat, he tries to kneel in back of Ma so it's harder for her to see—even though Ma doesn't miss too much.

After the rosary, we can sit our behinds down on our heels, but the prayers continue on and on—the acts of contrition and all the other acts. Then, if there are special things to pray for, and there usually are, there will be novenas for things like when somebody dies and we want to help them get into heaven in case they can't get there on their own. During Lent, the prayers stretch out even longer because that is the time when we all have to make up for all the sins that we did all year long, even though most of us go to confession almost every week. Maybe, everything hasn't been forgiven. It sure is easy to commit a sin when bad thoughts are thrown in as well as bad deeds.

About bad thoughts—one time, my brother Sam was so mean to me that I wished he was dead. Boy, did I have to make up to God for that one when Sam got hurt. Sam—we mostly call him Junior—stepped on a nail and had to have his large toe cut off. My mother and father made sure the toe was buried in holy ground because every part of a good Catholic has been blessed. All over the house it got pretty quiet for a change, except for a lot of praying. He was in the little bedroom on the first floor with its door opening out at the foot of the stairs into the dining room. Things got real bad when word came back that maybe his whole leg would have to be cut off. He had gotten gangrene. I made so many promises to God to make up for ever having wished he was dead. After all, it was probably my fault that he stepped on the nail in the first place. It's not only God who works in mysterious ways, but the devil is right there coaxing people to be bad at every turn. From then on, I sure tried to be much more careful about what I thought.

Well, back to the dining room. Our china cabinet sits between the window and the far wall. One day Rose and I were playing hide-and-seek. I was hiding under the china closet and Rose had just found me. Somehow, in all the fuss of push and pull, the whole cabinet came crashing down. It doesn't help to want to die. You can't just die on the spot. Of course my being the so-called "tomboy" and Rose being my mother's favorite, I was the one blamed for tipping it over.

I used to love looking at the pretty china things. Ma had managed to save up enough cornflakes and shredded wheat cereal box coupons over the years to get the china, one piece at a time, until at last there was a complete set of beautiful china. All the cream-colored dishes with a gold rim were so rich looking. I'll bet even city slickers don't have anything any prettier than that china. Our everyday dishes are mostly small metal plates and cups with chipped enamel.

The china closet held more than just beautiful china. On the top shelf was a clear, pale blue glass casserole dish with its own cover. Peeking out from under the cover were two dried roses. Their pink color with the green leaves looked so pretty against the blue of the dish. What made the roses so much more than just two beautiful roses is that they were a gift to my mother from Little Rose Ferron of Woonsocket, Rhode Island. Surely some day she will be canonized and beatified into a true saint. After all, Father Boyer, the pastor of our St. Edmund's Church in Ellenburg Center, is working very hard to make that happen. He has written a book about her and some miraculous things that have happened through her intercession, which means that she has prayed to God on behalf of people to help them get whatever they needed.

My mother and father treasured the roses and other relics that my mother got from Little Rose Ferron, who bore the stigmata of the cross on her hands and feet as well as bleeding wounds that replicated those made by Jesus' crown of thorns. Mostly those awful things happen to her about the same time of the year that Christ was crucified; but sometimes they happen to her at other times too. She offers her suffering to God for other people. Since my mother and father have been lucky enough to be able to actually visit Little Rose Ferron in Rhode Island a couple of times—I suppose at least the first time with Father Boyer's help—they have a very strong devotion to her. They are sure she is going to be a saint some day.

The front of the china closet had glass doors with narrow carved wood decorating its edges. It was all so pretty. My sister Rose is older than me by fifty-one weeks. She never gets blamed for anything, but I can't help but kind of like her.

She doesn't fight about anything like the length of the prayers, not taking showers with the other kids, all that kind of stuff. It doesn't even matter to me that she is so different from me. She actually likes taking piano lessons from our neighbor Miss Smith, even though she has to sit so long during the lesson and then has to practice at home on our piano after each lesson. My lessons and practicing the scales didn't last long even though the lessons were free. How could they last when animals—especially the horses—the woods, and all of nature that I love is outdoors?

There are other reasons I can't hate Rose. She seems to like me so much for what she calls my daredevil ways—everything from galloping horses to making matching slack suits for her and me from a pattern. My sewing started kind of funny. I hadn't sewn anything from a pattern—or much of anything else—on our foot-pedal Singer sewing machine. My mother didn't trust me to make her a dress with some very nice navy blue material she had. Finally, I managed to coax her into letting me make her the dress. I even put a nice white collar on it. She liked that dress and wore it a lot.

When Rose and I walk in the woods to pick berries, I make up and sing songs. She asks me how I know what I am singing. My answer is "I don't know," because I just make up words as I go along. We had a radio for only a few years. Dad listened to *Amos and Andy* and my mother listened to *Ma Perkins*. Of course, Dad listened to the news too. Finally, the bulb burned out in the radio and there just wasn't time or money to get the radio fixed. It sure would be wonderful if we could have music in the house instead of hollering.

4

Cold Winters ~ Ellenburg, N.Y., Farm

Winters are so bitter cold. Quite often it seems as if I can never get warm. Sometimes it's because the fire in the potbellied stove in school has just been started when we get there, or because, at home, the fire in the furnace or the fire in the kitchen stove has almost gone out. At about four o'clock in the morning, my father starts his day by building a fire in both the furnace and the kitchen stove. By that time of the morning, whatever wood he put in them before he went to bed is pretty much gone.

In the kitchen stove, he builds a fire by laying kindling wood on the bottom. Then he puts rather small pieces of split logs that are about eighteen inches long on top of the kindling. If there aren't a few glowing embers from the fire he built the night before, he uses some paper under the kindling to start the fire. In the furnace, a bigger chunk of wood has to be added to the kindling and the split logs to make the fire get bigger and last longer. Usually the logs have been split in half to make them easier to carry.

The furnace in our house is in the cellar. Over it is a heavy iron grate of one-inch squares covered with a coarse iron mesh that opens into the floor of the dining room. When the wood is even a little green or wet, the furnace sends out billowing clouds of smoke into the room. The smoke sometimes gets so bad that one of us has to open the door to let out smoke. Unfortunately, the near-zero-degree wind comes rushing in the door, so it usually gets closed real quick. The dining room ceiling over the furnace grate shows what happens when a lot of thick, dark gray smoke hits a white ceiling over and over again. During the winter, the spot keeps getting darker and darker until by spring it's quite gray.

I don't know why, but Ma always wants wet clothes just out of the washing machine first hung on a clothesline on the porch, even though a lot of the porch windows have been blown out by the north wind and it is bitterly cold outside.

There sure are frozen fingers for the person putting wet clothes on the porch clothesline. When the frozen clothes come back into the house, they are very stiff and funny looking. Dad's long underwear with the frozen arms and legs on top of the wooden bars of the wooden clothes rack, is enough to start Rose and me looking at each other and giggling, but we pretty much hid our giggles. After all, we might be considered bad if we got caught making fun of dads underwear. We put the clothes rack with its frozen clothes over the furnaces iron grate so the clothes can dry. It sure takes an awfully long time to dry clothes that way. It's as if summer will never come when we can hang wet clothes on the clothesline next to the playhouse.

In the middle of winter, there often is a howling whistling wind carrying its stinging load of snow that just doesn't ever stop its cry of freezing death. Sometimes, in the middle of the fury, we hear the crashing sound of a shattering porch window. I hate that sound. I so much want our house to look pretty like our neighbors, the Smiths. Each time another porch window comes crashing down, I know our house won't be pretty much longer. Maybe it's already not pretty, as the harsh wind has torn away, one at a time, most of the windows that enclosed most of the porch that frames the front of our house.

Dad tries, and I know he would fix the porch windows as they break if he had the time, but there are so many things that are more important—like milking cows, which starts at five o'clock in the morning and happens again at five o'clock in the evening. There are a whole lot of other chores, too, like feeding all of the animals morning and night, loading manure and spreading it over the fields, mending harnesses, shoeing horses, helping other farmers when a piece of their machinery breaks down, as well as fixing ours when they break down.

My father is the best of any farmer around at fixing broken machinery, and other things like making horseshoes. I'm very proud of my father for everything he does that other farmers don't seem to know how to do. Sometimes I hear my mother and father argue about what he fixes for other farmers when he hasn't done something for the house that she asked him to do a long time before and it still isn't done.

One thing that I find most embarrassing in the whole world is when the thirty-foot underground sewer line from our farmhouse to the cesspool freezes and backs the sewerage up to the holding tank under the washroom floor. Trying to find where the sewer line is frozen under frozen ground is an awful hard and nasty job that often leaves a messy ditch in the snow from the house to the cesspool in the middle of the lawn. I sure hope no neighbor ever sees that mess. After all, the house is a couple of hundred feet from the road and most of our neighbors aren't very friendly and don't visit. I think it has something to do with their either not being Catholic or not very good Catholics—like not going to church every Sunday—so my mother and father aren't very friendly with them either.

One particularly messy and smelly job on the farm is cleaning out manure in back of farm animals and then spreading it in the fields for fertilizer. We hitch a team of horses to a wagon manure spreader, which is shaped like a large box. The box is three feet wide by ten feet long and two and one-half feet deep. The box is set on a frame that has a set of wheels and a wooden tongue in front that the horses are hitched to. In the middle barn, where the manure is collected, there are two rows of cows with stanchions holding them so that their heads face the outside wall with its row of windows. Their behinds face a five-foot-wide cement walkway that is bordered on each edge with a foot-wide trough. The troughs are where most of the cows' poop ends up.

My father, my oldest brother Sam, or the hired man are the people who back the manure wagon along the walkway in back of the cows, then use a shovel to load the manure into the manure wagon. They drive the wagon out to the fields where the manure is spread with a fork over the fields for fertilizer. Sometimes in winter, when the snow is to deep the farmers leave the manure in an ever-growing pile somewhere near the barns. I sure feel awful when that happens at our farm and the pile starts getting higher and bigger in the field near the barn. When spring comes, the manure will have to be spread anyway. Besides, the Smiths, our closest neighbors, never have a manure pile, so it seems we should be able to do the same thing. When the men come into the house after spreading manure, it sure isn't hard to figure out what they have been doing. I wish there was a way to keep the manure smell out of the house.

All the farm chores do not leave much time for the men to do much of anything in the house. The milk from cows provides almost the only income to farm families, so all the men's attention goes to getting barn things done. One other thing that farmer's do is sell, for just a little bit of money, newborn calves that they think probably won't make good milking cows when they grow up. In addition, if there is a lot of hay in a season, then the farmers don't have to buy from each other.

My mother sometimes gets mad if she wants something real bad for the house, like a much-needed refrigerator, and we don't get it no matter how many years she waits. The only place we have to store things like milk, margarine, and salad dressing is the shelves at the top of the cellar steps. In the middle of summer, putting things on those shelves doesn't help very much to keep anything cool. When my father gets something like an extra piece of farm machinery that maybe he could do without (or maybe he could try to fix the old one), there sometimes is a pretty big fight. The farm things always come first.

I can't figure out whether my father is fair with my mother about things like that. We are always in debt, but, of course, our family always gives money in Saint Edmund's Catholic Church's Sunday collection and for special church drives. One time we gave $350. That was more money than our fancy Uncle Bill, who owns two farms, gave. On top of that, he is part owner of a store and has no kids. In a way, that made me very proud to give so much money, even though I get so unhappy when Ma and Dad argue so loud about things that have to do with money.

My father stands about five foot ten. He has blue eyes like mine. He's quite bald on top. The hair that is left is gray. His shoulders are a little rounded. I can remember when I was little and he carried me on his shoulders down the aisle in church. I was so proud. Most of the time my father is a rather quiet man who is always working very hard at chores of one kind or another.

Sunday is the only day that morning milking, feeding animals, and night milking are the only farm chores that are done. Of course, if it is summer and hay has been cut and is dry enough and it looks like its going to rain, the hay has to be brought into the barn whether it's Sunday or not. Something else that takes up most of Sunday is going to mass and sometimes confession for everybody. In the evening we're back on our knees for the rosary, acts of contrition, novenas, and special intentions. We sure don't get to play very much. During the summer, sometimes we do get to play softball with tennis balls that we get out of aunt Clarinda's Buffalo church clothing box. Or, in winter, we sometimes build snowhouses in snowdrifts.

I don't like fall very much. When I see snow fences going up on the sides of the road, I know it isn't going to be very long before an awful lot of snow and biting winter winds will be here. Snow always starts out so pretty, falling softly, leaving its white feathery blanket over the trees, the fields, the buildings—just everything. Snow can be such fun—first watching it fall and then playing in it. Or, it can be almost scary when it comes straight at me in what feels like needles with an icy shrill whistling sound. For a couple of months after the snow starts falling, snowplows are pretty good at keeping the roads clear so horses, sleds, and cars can use them. Through November, and later in December, the snowbanks on the sides of the roads made by snowplows keep getting higher and higher.

The snow fences that are placed forty feet back from the road and have four- to five-foot snowdrifts in front of them do keep some snow from getting to the road. That isn't enough to keep the piercing wind from blowing a lot of snow over the already six- or seven-foot snowbanks on the side of the road. Finally, by January and February, there is just too much snow between the snowbanks on each side of the road, and the snowplows can't push any more snow from the middle of the road to the top of the snowbanks. In our area, there is only one huge snowblower. It is attached to a truck body and it chews up snow and spits it over the side of the snowbanks. We don't see that blower very often. Ours is a dirt road that almost never sees fancy equipment. Sometimes, even when the driver of the snowblower truck does try to clear our road, he just can't. The snow is packed too hard, and the snowbanks are just too high.

Making a snowhouse in a snowdrift next to the snow fence never works very well. If we kids dig a three-by-two-foot snowhouse out of a five-foot-high snowdrift, it usually caves in after a couple of visits of the kids, if it doesn't collapse while we're making it. The ten-foot-high, hard-packed snowbank on the side of the road is a much better place to build a snowhouse, but they are scary to make and to play in. There always should be at least two kids—one kid looking out for cars and snowplows and the other one digging out the snow. Of course, the whole thing is a sin because we have been told, in no uncertain terms, to never make a snowhouse in one of these snowbanks.

For at least one month each winter, the only way to get to the main east/west road one mile away from our house is to walk or go by horse and sled. Every once in a while in winter, I get to do something I love. I hitch up the small gray horse Kit to a one-horse cutter, then let my brothers and sisters try to hang onto the sleds they tie to the back of the cutter. The game is for me to try and upset their sleds whatever way I can. Sometimes I can upset them by galloping peppy Kit or by running the edge of the sleigh a short way up the snowbank on the sides of the road. It sure is wonderful to hear joyful laughter; there is so little of it on any farm I know of.

When the temperature is well below zero, the snow becomes so hard packed that it creaks under our boots. By late January, it feels as if summer will never ever come. We always have short, bitterly cold, snow-laden days with piercing winds. In addition, there are cranky, quarrelling kids and parents. And, in the barns, there are suffering cows, heifers, and calves that haven't been let out all winter. One of the worst things about winter is sometimes hearing my father's mumbled voice and seeing his drawn face when he talks about our hay and oat supply that may not last through the rest of the winter. Cows give less milk in winter, and our milk checks keep getting smaller and smaller as the months go by. Our animal and people food bills keep getting bigger and bigger.

My father and oldest brother Sam are very hardworking farmers. Dad and Sam, at one time, tried making more money by working at a mine in Lyon Mountain many miles away while still working the farm. In the very early morning, they got up to build fires in the furnace and in the kitchen stove, then went to the barn to feed the animals and milk the cows. After hitching up a horse to a sleigh, they rode over snowbanks to the horse shed in Ellenburg Center next to Uncle Bill's store where they left the horse. The shed is open to outside on its west side. From the store, they got a ride back and forth to the Lyon Mountain mine. Sam worked in the mine. Dad worked as a carpenter helping to build houses for the mining company.

Lyon Mountain was where my mother's brother Ed was very badly hurt. For many years, he suffered through endless major and minor operations. No wonder he was such a grouch. I sure would have liked it if he had talked to me even a little bit, but instead he wouldn't even look at me. It was as if he didn't like me at all. He didn't talk to my brothers and sisters either. I wonder if it bothered them. In our family, we don't talk about things like that. When he wasn't around at my grandmother's house, ever so often we would hear that he was in a hospital having another operation, or that he was in Florida on a vacation that the mine paid for.

I couldn't wait to get to the sled when Dad and Sam got back from the mine. We kept a black cowhide blanket in the sled that we used to cover the horse when it was left in the horse shed or to cover whoever was riding in the sled. With the little extra money Dad earned, he often splurged and bought cookies. There would be a wonderful ten-pound bag of assorted cookies hidden underneath the blanket. He would unhitch the horse and, as soon as Dad, Sam, and the horse disappeared inside the barn door, I would go to find the bag of cookies that held my second most favorite cookies in the entire world after Toll House cookies—vanilla wafers. There weren't any other fancy cookies, and there weren't many vanilla wafers. I didn't have much time before somebody would come back into the carriage house, so I really had to hurry. Taking those cookies was probably a venial sin, not a mortal sin, so it was sure worth it. Besides, I could tell that in confession, so even if I died before confession, I'm pretty sure the worst I would get was purgatory before going to heaven.

The Lyon Mountain second jobs did not last very long. The mountain was many miles away and the farm chores—night and morning—were just too much for Dad and Sam, even though there was the never-ending pressure of the wintertime milk checks that were so small. The milk checks never keep up with even the bare necessities for our family. If the summer has been very rainy or very dry, sometimes Dad has to buy hay from the GLF, the feed store at Ellenburg Depot, before spring. During the summer months, there is an almost frantic scramble to try and pay off at least some of the past winter bills from the little bit more money that comes in the summer checks.

As our family keeps getting bigger, it gets harder and harder to buy things like cereal, flour, sugar, and salt that doesn't come from living on a farm—and clothes, even though we sometimes get big boxes of clothes from Aunt Clarinda's Buffalo, New York, parish clothing drive. Most of the Buffalo church ladies and their kids must be pretty darn small. Almost all the clothes are too small for us big farm kids. Nobody in our family is fat, but we sure aren't skinny either. Ma and Dad talk a lot about not getting much money for milk and needing things. Sometimes they talk in voices I can barely hear even if I try real hard. One time, I heard them talk about maybe some of us kids might have to go to some kind of a home or orphanage. That sure is very scary. I wonder if I would be one of those kids. Maybe not, since I get the cows out of the pasture on horseback and do the raking of hay in summertime and help with the milking in the evening. I have some bad dreams about maybe being one of those kids.

Sometimes things aren't so nice for big people. Sometimes things aren't so nice for kids, either.

5

Aunt Cora and Uncle Ed

Aunt Cora is the wife of my Uncle Ed Patnode, my father's brother. Aunt Cora isn't very tall. Her hair is gray and tied back in a bun. It seems as if she never takes off her apron. It has a bib that goes to the back of her neck and ties in back at the waist. Both the apron and her dress are always colorful cotton prints of flowers or checks. She wears black leather shoes that lace in the front and have two-inch-square, one-and-one-half-inch-high rubber heels like the shoes that nuns wear. Their farm is about a mile away from our farm. Aunt Cora is such a nice person. She doesn't say much, and, when she does, it is so soft you can barely hear what she says. She is always cooking or cleaning. Aunt Cora does her chores very quietly and with no complaints—at least not any I ever hear. Uncle Ed is a little over six feet tall and my cousins, their farmer sons, are all almost six feet tall, if not taller. Aunt Cora always has their meals ready on the table when they come in from the evening milking.

The men come into the house through a door in the woodshed where they take off their high rubber outer boots and hang their farm jackets on hooks. Inner felt boots are what they wear in the house. They use a hand pump at the kitchen sink to get water into an enamel basin for washing up before they sit down to a meal. Boy, this family is sure quiet compared to my family, where, at every meal, a couple of kids and my mother always seem to be talking or hollering about something or other. Dinner at Aunt Cora's is almost always pretty quiet. After dinner, Uncle Ed sits in his rocking chair by the kitchen window and my men cousins sit in plain-back or rocking chairs in the middle room that has a potbellied stove. The stove has a little isinglass window in the door on its side. Isinglass is mica that comes from the ground and can be made into little thin, see-through windows for stoves.

The only water in the house comes from the hand pump in the kitchen sink. The sink is made of iron and is quite black. It is about three feet long by one and one-half feet wide and four inches deep. The iron sink is set into a wooden frame with the metal pump resting on the wooden frame at one end with the mouth of the pump over the sink and the pump handle over the wood frame. The pump first has to be primed by pouring water into the pump's body then pumping the handle up and down until water gushes from its mouth. The spurts of water come at the same time as the pumping of the handle. Push down, spurt, up again, over and over again. Even though I would like to help pump water for Aunt Cora, I feel too embarrassed to say much of anything to anybody except in my own house. I don't know why I feel like that with Aunt Cora. She seems so nice.

At Aunt Cora's and my house nobody ever says nice things to each other or says nice things about other people. There are only certain things, like school, that I talk about with my brothers and sisters. I have to be careful that something isn't repeated in a way I didn't mean or changed enough to be considered something bad. Some of my brothers and sisters are tattletales. Nobody talks about what they think about different topics—like boys, or whether we like or dislike something our mother or father does. Maybe other kids tell each other things that I don't know anything about.

Aunt Cora's meals are pretty much the same as ours except that everybody gets as much as they want to eat no matter what time of the year it is. The meat is beef or pork—very seldom chicken—with potatoes, boiled or baked. Chickens have to be saved to lay eggs. Sometimes there is a second vegetable like beans or corn, or, in the summer, fresh tomatoes. Of course, the men are always served first, but that doesn't really matter. She always has wonderful meals and she does give us second helpings. Often there is a dessert of cake, cookies, or a pie, which we sure don't get nearly as often at our house. Boy, they sure don't talk to each other very much. At my house it's always noisy.

At our house, when a cow gets too old to give very much milk, which is about eight or nine years old, she is killed for food. And pigs, when they get to be a couple hundred pounds, are killed for us to eat. I expect that's pretty much what other farmers do too. I don't think farmers talk to each other very much, but I expect that has to do with their not getting together for much of anything besides threshing oats. For instance, I never hear my father or my brothers using our hand-cranked, party-line telephone. Ma gets mad if she catches us listening in on another family's phone conversation. Every once in a while, something very interesting is whispered about that one of us heard while listening on our party line. After all, sometimes when we go to use the phone, there already is somebody on the line, and who can help listening for at least a minute or two?

Nobody says nice things about pigs. They are the only farm animal that I know of that, if they have enough room, potty on one side of their pen and eat and sleep on the other side. In the summer, it is fun to find fat, three-foot-tall pigweeds and take them to the pigs in their pen outdoors next to the east side of the barn. They grunt mightily as they gobble up the weeds. I like the pigs a lot. Little pigs are so cute and squeaky. I hate thinking about how they end up on our kitchen table.

At night at Uncle Ed's, the family prayers are awfully short compared to the evening prayers of my family. Most of my cousins don't even kneel during prayers. At their house, I can rest my behind on my heels as I kneel. I don't think any of my cousins or my aunt or uncle would say anything if I didn't kneel at all, but whatever sister is with me might very well tell Ma and then what? Their kitchen is very big and homey. There is a large, seven-foot, round wooden table in the middle of the floor. Around the table are six heavy wooden chairs. A rocker used by Uncle Ed is near a window on the east side of the room. It looks quite comfortable, but, of course, we never sit in it. It is Uncle Ed's chair.

I don't know how Aunt Cora gets Uncle Ed and my boy cousins, when they are getting ready to go to the barn to do chores, to first put on felt under boot in the house and then their regular high rubber boots in the woodshed. When they come back from the barn, they leave their rubber outer boots in the woodshed, which saves mud and cow manure from being brought into the house. Maybe she doesn't have to tell them because they just know without being told.

Farm families don't visit very much, even when people are relatives. There are all kinds of chores for the parents and usually for most of the kids, so I don't get to see Uncle Ed and his family except when I ride a horse to their house. I think that maybe in our family there is another reason that my father doesn't seem very close to any of his ten brothers and sisters. By the time my father started a family with my mother, who is eighteen years younger than he is, my father's parents were both dead. Over the years, I've heard nice things about both of my grandparents and that there was some kind of trouble between my father and his brothers and sisters when their parents died and my father took over the family farm in Ellenburg.

I don't know how this happened, but on one of my visits to Aunt Cora's and Uncle Ed's house, I burned the back of the fingers of my right hand. It was so nice to be fussed over. Of course, the first thing they put on my burn was butter. I didn't cry much. I am a farm kid and tears are for sissy city kids. I sure am not a sissy.

Whenever I can manage, I coax my father into letting me go to Uncle Ed's house and then coax my sister Rose to go with me. When the answer is yes, I bridle up two horses. I always take the horse that is most likely to act up because

Rose is a bit of a sissy. That means it is probably small, gray Kit for her and big, wild Ned for me. During the summer, I ride bareback every day getting cows from the pasture to our farm. To get the cows, I usually use Kit, but if I'm feeling more daring, I take Ned, which is why Rose seems to think I'm very daring.

Sometimes I show off by drawing a horse to a quick stop, moving the bridle lines forward, and throwing my right leg over the horse's mane with a mighty flourish. Or, when I'm several hundred feet from the barn, I let the cows get ahead of me, then let the horse out at a full gallop. I love galloping horses, but I'm usually worried about making them too tired. I have to make sure to slow down just before getting back to the low entrance to the barn, or the horse will gallop right into the barn and knock me off its back.

Aunt Cora and Uncle Ed's house has no inside plumbing. We have two bath-rooms and inside plumbing. Yet, at our house, things always seem so mixed up, with kids being loud and running around without my mother knowing what to do. At Aunt Cora's, everything is quiet and they don't even have running water or inside plumbing. Maybe there are a lot of things kids don't know.

The two-seater at Uncle Ed's house is some distance from the kitchen door. To get to the outhouse, you start at the kitchen door and take a twenty-five-foot-long pathway through the woodshed past neatly stacked split wood to the door of the outhouse. The outhouse is a small shed attached to the southwest corner of the woodshed. In the middle of winter, the howling wind sends it's grasping chill through the flimsy walls. I sure hurry, but it's hard to potty when my behind is on one of the two toilet holes in freezing cold wood. For toilet paper, there is a small frigid pile of magazines and newspapers. If I have to go in the middle of the night, there are chamber pots under the bed. A pot with no cover is for number one, and a pot with a cover is for number two. I sure can tell by the noise of the ceramic pot cover if anybody is using the number two pot. None of us empties chamber pots. Aunt Cora never says anything, and, even if I thought I should be emptying a pot, the whole thing is just too embarrassing to say anything.

There are two ways to get to Uncle Ed's house. The longer way is along the road, so most of the time we go the shorter route through the Trombley farm fields. I'm not sure how they feel about our using their quarter-mile, dirt drive-way, then to the back of their house and their fields to get to a blacktop road for the rest of the trip to Uncle Ed's. We never see a woman around the farmhouse or in the fields, but we sometimes see a man and kids around, so I guess there is a woman in the family. Sometimes farmwives don't leave the farm more than once or twice a year. Nobody ever stops us or comes out of the house or barn to say anything, so I guess it's all right. I often wonder what it would be like inside the house and barn.

Except for the time I got burned, the stove in the middle room of my aunt and uncle's house is such a comfort. It is a four-foot-high, black potbellied affair on rather small feet. The stove's figured and curved top is on hinges and can be turned aside, leaving a flat metal surface covering the flames below. Aunt Cora keeps a kettle of water on the top of the stove to add moisture to the very dry winter air. The door that opens on the front of the belly of the stove is on hinges and has a small isinglass window.

On our farm on the side of the mountain near the day pasture, is a hole in the ground that is about twelve feet across and five feet deep. We were told that it was a hole dug to see if the isinglass in the ground was of a high enough grade to mine. Isinglass is mica in thin translucent sheets. I looked that up in a dictionary at school. I wonder what our life would have been like if a good grade of isinglass had been found, but, since the hole was dug long before we were born, maybe we wouldn't have been born at all. Dancing red-orange flames licking at round logs are almost always visible through the little isinglass window in the stove.

Like at our house, before they go out to do barn chores at four or five o'clock in the morning, the men stock the potbellied and kitchen stoves so they will burn for many hours. Mostly Aunt Cora adds wood to the stoves during the day, especially if the kitchen oven needs to be hot for baking. In late evening, the men are the ones who set up the stoves with wood for overnight burning. There is a daybed and various chairs, both rocking and straight backed, in the middle room, together with a couple of small end tables and lamps. There is a bookcase against the wall on the east side of the room with paneled glass doors.

There is one room in Uncle Ed's house that gives me some of the same feeling that the mysterious forest on our farm does. The forest is on top of our little Adirondack mountain to the east of the day pasture and doesn't have old trees because they were all cut down years ago for firewood. New trees, about fifteen feet high, grow so close together that there is very little sunshine peeking through the green leaves, and only layers of dead leaves cover the dark earth along with infrequently seen small snakes and porcupines. Cows almost never go into the mysterious forest.

In Uncle Ed's house, the mysterious room is the parlor with its lingering smell of furniture polish. A set of glass-paneled doors leads from the north side of the middle room to the seldom-used parlor. The room's special treasure is a beautifully kept and almost-never-used player piano. In the piano bench are rolls of different tunes. Uncle Ed's kids are older than most of the kids in my family. If only my family had a player piano. None of us Sam Patnode kids is ever allowed to touch that wonderful piano. I would be very careful, but I'm not sure about some of my brothers and sisters. Sometimes my older cousin Irene plays the piano for us. It seems almost like magic when the dancing white keys jump up and down by themselves as she pumps the foot pedals underneath.

One time, Uncle Ed bought me white snow boots. No matter what, I know I will love him till I die. With our family being poor and there being so many kids, you sure don't get to be special very often. There are from fifteen to twenty kids in grades one through six in our one-room schoolhouse. It is so very exciting to be able to wear the boots to school, even though my beautiful boots are not very warm because only one pair of socks fits inside them with my feet. They have laces up the front and go several inches above my ankle. I'm sure I must be one of his favorites or he would never have bought me boots that made me feel so special. I shall never forget the boots—or him. I don't know why my father doesn't seem to get along very well with Uncle Ed, and I think it has something to do with his brothers and sisters before he married my mother. I haven't been able to find out anything else.

Sometimes I go into Uncle Ed's barn. Their cows are so pretty and always look fat and clean no matter what time of the year it is. Most of them have big reddish orange patches on white. All of our cows are black and white. During the winter, I'm pretty sure he even lets them out every day. One of the reasons he might be able to do that is because he has more than one older son to help out on his farm.

My Uncle Ed got a prize bull and is working at building up a prize herd. I wonder what Aunt Cora thinks about all the things I'm telling you. After all, they get their money the same way we get ours—milk from their cows. There never seems to be a question at their house the way there is at ours as to whether the mother gets something for the house or the father gets something for the barn. I guess that must not be a question at their house with Aunt Cora so quiet and her not having inside plumbing like we do.

All the farmers work so hard. I wonder if they will get rewards in heaven even if they don't go to church or if they are mean to their wives, kids, and animals. Maybe they will go to confession just before they die if they did bad things and everything will turn out okay no matter what.

6

Neighbors ~ Mr. and Mrs. George Smith

Mrs. Smith is a lot like my Aunt Cora. They are both quiet ladies who wear cotton printed dresses over which they wear aprons that have bibs that go over their heads and an apron front that goes to the bottom of their dresses. The apron edges are finished with bias binding, and there are ties in back at the waist. Their stockings are always a tan color, and their shoes are always black leather that lace in front and have two-inch-square, one-and-one-half-inch-high rubber heels. They are both a little plump and about five feet two inches tall with long gray hair pulled into a bun.

Mr. and Mrs. Smith's house is only a quarter mile away from ours. They are our closest neighbors. The Smiths have only one kid, whose name is Iris. She is the home economics teacher at Ellenburg Corner High School. They live in the same kind of a house as my Aunt Cora. Neither house has running water, so, of course, there is no inside plumbing.

At our house and all the other farms around us, we use the wood cut from trees in our cow pastures to heat our houses, warm water, and cook meals. In the winter, the farmers, after finishing the morning milking and feeding the animals, often hitch a team of their strongest horses to a sled, which they use for hauling wood from the forest. The sled is a wooden, flatbed frame with two sets of runners, one for the front and one for the back. Between the sets of runners, the sleds are made so the back part can move right or left from the front part. No matter how deep the snow is, rocks and tree stumps often stick out from the snow, so the path down the mountain and to the farm building often is not a very straight one.

To fell a tree, first Dad and my brother Sam or our hired man make a straight cut halfway into the trunk about two feet from the ground. The size of the tree determines how deep the cut will be—the bigger the tree, the deeper the cut. The cut is made on the side of the tree that is where Dad wants the tree to fall. The usual size of our trees requires a cut of about six to eight inches. Next, another cut is made at an angle down into the straight cut. The two cuts remove a wedge of wood from the tree. For the third cut, they use a two-man saw to cut into the tree on the opposite side of the bottom cut of the wedge.

The two-man saw has a wooden handle on each end. The men pull the blade back and forth until the tree starts to tremble a little at the top, and the trunk is nearly cut through. That's the time when everybody needs to be especially careful. Sometimes trees don't fall exactly where they're expected to fall. We are careful to never stand close to the tree where the wedge has been cut. When the tree starts to shiver it will be just a matter of a minute or two before it falls over.

Watching trees being cut down always makes me feel bad. I like trees a lot. One minute there it is a wonderful, big tree reaching into the sky, and the next minute it is being cut until it gently sways before gathering speed with a wrenching scream on the way down until it hits the ground with a thunderous crash. It always makes me feel particularly sad to see maple trees cut down. These are maple trees that have given us sap in early spring for wonderful maple syrup. Every kid tries to use the biggest share of this yummy treat with bread and butter or for pancakes.

After a tree is cut down, I count the life rings from the outside to the center of the stump so I can tell how old it was. They are always older than I—how sad. Their rustling leaves are so green in summer as they make part of heaven's roof along with the puffy white clouds scattered among the powder blue sky. Their trunks quite often hold a chipmunk nest where we can see little chipmunk baby faces peeping out of their little home. I don't think the farm men or my brothers or sisters ever give any of this much thought. On our farm there is a retreating tree line that, each year as the trees are cut down, is advancing closer to the top of the mountain. The remaining sentry tree stumps act as tombstones for the majesty that was.

Back to our neighbors, the Smiths. Mrs. Smith has the same kind of two-seater outhouse as my Aunt Cora and it's pretty much in the same place in the house. I always try to use one of the two bathrooms with running water back at our house before I go to the Smith's.

In the unheated workroom that is just off the kitchen, are two large metal tubs. I think one of the things they are used for is taking a bath. Of course I really don't know because you can be sure that when any of the Smiths is going to take a bath I just know he or she would make sure that none of us kids was in their house. I do know that the tubs are used for washing clothes because I sometimes see Mrs. Smith move the wet clothes from one tub to the other. I don't know why, but washing clothes is something she never asks me to help her with. All the water for the house comes from a hand pump mounted on the end of a large metal pan on legs. The pump is a lot like the one at Aunt Cora's house. The pan is about ten inches deep, one and one-half feet wide, and three feet long. It's on the north wall in the kitchen next to the door to the washroom. I sure wouldn't mind pumping out a lot of water for her to do things like the laundry, but she never asks me.

On the east wall of Mrs. Smith's kitchen are two windows that open and close from the middle. There are beautiful, fluffy yellow kitchen curtains with tiebacks at the top of the windows, and curtains that hang straight down at the bottom of the window. The inside and bottom edges of the curtains have ruffled edges. There are cacti and other strange-looking, small potted plants on the windowsills as well as on the ledge in the middle of the window where the top and bottom come together. Sometimes, there is a vine hanging from the top of the window. In the morning, the sun shines through and dances around all the beautiful yellow and green of plants and curtains. I sure wish we had pretty things like that back at our house.

Mrs. Smith is the sweetest, kindest woman in the whole world. Sometimes I am the lucky one who gets to clean her house on Saturday for one dollar. I'm kind of proud that none of my sisters is ever asked to clean the Smith house. I sure like the idea that maybe it's because she likes me more than any of my sisters. Being asked to clean their house does not happen nearly as often as I'd like.

I'm saving that money and the five cents a bushel we get for picking up newly dug potatoes in the fall in order to have five dollars to send to African missionaries. Our parents encourage us kids to give the five dollars to our parish priest so he can send the money to Africa because that's how much it takes to save a soul over there.

Mrs. Smith has all kinds of flowers, like roses, hollyhocks, and green shrubs that make lovely borders around the house and around the lawn. The lawn is always kept mowed to the perfect height of about three inches with a hand-pushed mower. I love the look. I so much want our big lawn to look the same—short green grass with beautiful shrubs and flowers around the house. I want to be proud of how our house looks, but my mother doesn't seem able to get her kids—me and my brothers and sisters—organized, so getting things done like mowing the lawn or washing the dishes always seems to end in a fight. Often the words ring out getting louder and louder as kids got madder, "It's your turn!" "No, it's *your* turn!"

I so much want our house to look like Mrs. Smith's that I often dream I keep the lawn mowed. In real life, I only get one-third to one-half of the lawn in front of the house done before it is too dark to mow or I have to do something else. My real wish is to not only have the big yard in the front of the house mowed, but also the yards at the west side and the back of the house with its very small orchard of crab apple and apple trees. All that mowing would take a long time, but the house would look so beautiful.

When I go to Mrs. Smith's to clean, I am never asked to water the plants. Actually, I'm kind of glad about that. What if I gave them a lot more water than they should have, or maybe not enough? I sure would feel awful if something bad happened to them. I clean the rooms. The second floor is a good place to start. The bedrooms all seem so perfect, with very similar furnishings and already look- ing very clean. The floors are beautiful hardwood maple with small handmade scatter rugs here and there. The rugs are made from torn strips of old clothes tied together then braided and sewn into flat oval shapes of different sizes. The beds are covered with handmade quilts of small squares or triangles of many different colors and patterns, all edged in one to two feet of a solid color.

The bedrooms each have a straight-backed wooden chair without arms and with a small cushion on the seat. There is a small dresser with a mirror, and a small, two-drawer, low chest that holds a plain, white ceramic pitcher sitting in a matching washbasin. All the rooms in the house, including Mr. and Mrs. Smith's on the first floor, have matching pitchers and washbasins. With no bathrooms with running water, people who sleep in the bedrooms need to be able to wash up in their rooms. I give the same cleaning to the rooms that nobody sleeps in: a slightly damp mop for dusting the floor, and a clean cloth dampened with a bit of oil to dust the heavy, dark, wooden furniture.

The parlor in the southwest corner of the house is even less used than Aunt Cora's parlor. In fact, I can't remember anyone in the room except me doing a quick dusting. The much-more-used room on the southeast side of the house is at the foot of the stairs. On the far wall are French doors that are the entrance to the parlor. The room has a daybed and a much-treasured piano where Iris, the Smith's daughter, gives my sister Rose piano lessons.

In the Smith's house, the room at the foot of the stairs where the piano is has a west wall that continues as one side of a hall that leads to Mrs. and Mrs. Smith's bedroom on the left and on to the kitchen with a pantry on the same side. I love the pantry with its large jars of doughnuts and cookies. Mrs. Smith makes the most wonderful doughnuts in the whole wide world. She is generous and, even after she gives me one doughnut, she often offers me a second one. Usually I am too embarrassed to say yes to a second doughnut. She might think less of me. I don't know why that idea pops in my head—it just does. Being embarrassed so easily sure is something I wish didn't happen.

Sometimes I have a lucky day, which doesn't happen very often because Mrs. Smith doesn't help with barn chores. On these lucky days, she takes a trip to the barn nearby for extra milk or eggs. Thank goodness there is a window in the pantry. She might not tell me she's going to the barn, but when I hear something that sounds like a door closing I take a quick look out the pantry window. I have to wait until I'm sure she is on her way to the barn and hasn't forgotten something back at the house. Quick, quick, can I snitch one or two? It depends on how many are in the jar, and if I can move them around enough so she doesn't notice my snitching. I wonder if it's a sin. Every once in a while I almost get caught. With the actual snitch itself, then the cover-up, then stuffing down the treats, I sure have to hurry. How can I ask for another doughnut if I already said no thanks to a second one? I wonder if somehow she knows when I take an extra doughnut or two. Whenever there are cookies or doughnuts or cake at my house, they disappear in such a hurry, it's almost as if they were never there.

The kitchen is a rather fat L-shape. Mr. Smith's easy chair, which is never to be used by anyone else, is on the north side between the pantry door and the wood-burning stove. The wood-burning part of the stove is on the left side and a water reservoir is on the right, with an oven door in the front that is hinged on the bottom so it can be pulled down. That stove is very much like the one we have at our house. It is the shape of a large metal box about four feet wide by two feet from front to back. There are six round, nine-inch, removable iron plates in the flat top with a sheet of metal rising from the back for about two feet, which holds a warming closet at the top of the stove. The warming closet has a lid that can be pushed open. It holds things like warming serving dishes and cooked food. Between Mr. Smith's chair and the stove, there is a wooden box that holds the wood to be burned.

The window next to his chair has the same wonderful yellow pull-back curtain on top with panels on the bottom.

Across from Mr. Smith's chair is a daybed that has a cushion seat and a couple of small pillows. Next to it is a small end table that holds a lot of wonderful magazines that I'm not allowed to look at like *Life* and the *Saturday Evening Post*. The furniture is well worn, but so neatly kept that I have only warm cozy feelings when I'm in the kitchen. In the parlor and the upstairs rooms I always feel a little uneasy. My very big family is neither neat nor quiet. God, I love quiet. Mrs.

Smith does talk a little, but it is always in a soft and gentle tone. At my house, on many occasions, if I am to be heard at all, I practically have to scream.

I so love Mrs. Smith, who is so quiet and always treats me so nicely. I think that somehow she knows my mother and father think that most people, especially Protestants, need to be watched very carefully. Our Catholic Church sees bad things coming from so many different directions. Of course, this includes evil in thoughts and certainly in deeds. Even though the Smiths are Protestants, I just know they are going to go to heaven when they die. They are too good to go anywhere else.

Mrs. Smith has a wonderful set of books about the Bobbsey twins. I quickly read through the whole set of books that she loaned me one at a time. Those books and some other books are in the bookcase just to the left as you come into the kitchen from the porch. On the right side is the sturdy wooden kitchen table and chairs, which are in front of the windows with all the wonderful plants and curtains. That's where the first rays of the sun come in from the east to lighten the long, bitterly cold winter days.

I'm finding it hard to talk about the cellar with its forbidden wonders, which Mrs. Smith probably understands I so desperately want to share. She saves the *Saturday Evening Post* and *Life* magazines after she reads them. They are stored in the cellar. I think the *Saturday Evening Post* might be allowed by my mother, but I don't dare ask because—who knows?—she might stop me from going to the Smiths'. I sure know from hearing things around the house that the scandalous *Life* is definitely a sinful magazine. I heard that sometimes it has pictures of people with hardly any clothes on. One time, I told my mother about seeing a *Life* magazine at Mrs. Smith's. She called Mrs. Smith to tell her that I was forbidden from ever seeing any magazines. Somehow, I managed to let Mrs. Smith know I would never talk about it again so that "angel woman" trusted me, and I had a few more visits to her cellar.

One chore that actually does bother me is ironing Mr. and Mrs. Smith's daughter Iris's slips. She is the high school's home economics teacher, and somehow I really don't like ironing her satin slips using the flatiron heated on the wooden stove. I think I am unhappy about ironing her slips because she has so much education, while nobody in my family has even started moving to such an important social place—and then to think she wears ironed slips that have been ironed by me! I sure don't mind ironing shirts, dresses, pants, aprons, or whatever, but Iris's slips?

Of course, I would never say anything about that to Mrs. Smith. She might think I wasn't so nice and maybe even not want me at her house anymore. That sure would make me feel awful.

7

My Father and Mr. Smith

I don't know why, but we kids always call our neighbor "Mrs. Smith." I guess it's probably because we all like her so much. But with her husband, Mr. Smith, it's different. When we talk about him we sometimes say "George Smith." And when we're talking about their daughter, we say "Iris." Of course, whenever we are talking in front of our mother or father, the Smiths themselves, or Iris, the Smiths are "Mr. and Mrs. Smith" and Iris is "Miss Smith." In addition, we would never dare or even want to call Iris anything but Miss Smith to her face. After all, she's important. She's a home economics teacher in the Ellenburg High School.

George Smith seems so different from Mrs. Smith. Maybe it's because he chews tobacco. That alone sure makes me like Mrs. Smith more than I like Mr. Smith. Of course, when I spend time with her when I clean her house, I get to know what a very nice person she is. I guess chewing tobacco is what left him with almost no teeth in the front of his mouth, and the ones that are left, darkened to almost black. That part isn't the worst. After all, I don't have to look at his face. But the spittle that comes from chewing tobacco is something else. In the house, next to his favorite chair, is a spittoon. I don't have to look when he is spitting into the spittoon, but I sure can't stop the squishy sound he makes when he's spitting.

Sometimes it is impossible to not see him spitting when we are riding in his car. It doesn't happen very often, but I'm sure all anybody has to do is hear and see the spitting once to never forget. The car is moving, he opens the car window, and, if the wind happens to be blowing in the wrong direction, a trail of brown spittle runs down the part of the car window that hasn't been cranked down. Of course, there is no way that the spittle will be cleaned off before we get back to his house. Another thing that happens when he is squirting out long brown streams is that a little bit of the spittle always seems to stay around the corners of his mouth. At least he doesn't use his sleeves to wipe off his mouth like some of the other farmers do. But he, like Mrs. Smith, is a very gentle person. I wonder what

Mrs. Smith thinks about his chewing tobacco. I never hear her say anything about it, and I sure wouldn't dare ask.

It is the practice of almost all the local farmers to cut off the horns of the animals that are going to grow up to be milking cows. When they are just getting old enough to be called heifers, and the horns are about four inches long, they are cut off. The cutting is so awful. It takes several farmers to do the job. It takes at least one to hold the heifer that is desperately trying to get away from the cutting, and one farmer to do the actual sawing off of the horns. The heifers let out the most awful, agonized, long bellows of pain that go right through me. I so hate and dread to hear that awful sound and sure go back to the house in a hurry when the cutting starts. The sight left after the cutting breaks my heart. What's left is a round, thick rim of bone where the horns have been cut close to the head so they won't grow back. In the center of the rim of bone is a small crater weeping bloody oozing matter.

George Smith never cuts his cows' horns. The horns grow from about eight to twelve inches long. His mostly Holstein cows usually are slow moving and gentle but, of course, even cows have boss cows and cows that follow the boss cow. It probably was a boss cow playing around in the rock-strewn Smith's night pasture that got too frisky, and with an upward thrust, slit open the belly of another cow. That story came up with the yearly cuttings in order to shut up anybody who said anything about the awful cutting of heifers' horns.

Mr. Smith has other ways of showing what a nice man he is. Most of the farmers keep their cows tied in their stanchions for all of the bitter cold winter months from the middle of October to springtime when enough new grass has started to peek through the newly thawed earth for the cows to start to graze. George Smith doesn't do that. Almost every day, even when the snow has blown into a pile in front of the barn doors and has to be shoveled away, no matter how much extra work it is, he lets his cows out of the barn. When cows are let out every day, the area outdoors where they move around forms a circle of trampled snow and mud. The circle keeps getting smaller and smaller as the winter drags on and the snow gets deeper. I don't know how he does it. His animals are always neat and tidy year round without manure caked to their backsides even though he has only one hired man and himself to work the farm.

Other farmers often have two or three sons, and sometimes daughters, helping, and most don't keep their farm and animals as nice as Mr. Smith does. Some of the wives from the back roads are kept almost as slaves working in both the houses and the barns. One woman comes out only once a year to go to the store for flour and sugar. None of us has ever seen the wife from another neighboring farm going past our house—only the men and boys of the family. Farmers and their families get to know the people who go past their farms from their horses, sleds, or wagons, or, in summer, maybe an old truck. For farmers living east of us, there is no other road than the one past our house to get their milk delivered to Ellenburg Center.

A one-horse sleigh called a cutter sure comes in handy when we are snowed in all the way to the blacktop county road one mile away. The sleigh is a great way to get somebody to a Greyhound bus going through the Ellenburgs or Uncle Ed's store in Ellenburg Center. Sometimes on a Sunday we use it for fun or a trip to St. Edmund's Catholic Church four miles away. Four miles each way in a cutter is a pretty long way and doesn't happen very often even though there is a shelter for horses at church. The first floor of a two-story hall next to the church has a dirt floor, and the side facing the street is open to outdoors. Horses can be tied up inside while people go to church.

The second floor of this hall is used for a yearly church affair and sometimes for square dances. The church affair is a place where there are a lot of people, and, for once, we kids aren't watched too closely. That's probably because I can't imagine how a kid could get into very much mischief. There is bingo with all kinds of different prizes, a wheel on which people put money down hoping that the little slapping rubber hand will stop on their number, housewives' home-prepared food like potato salad, coleslaw, pies, cakes, and cookies. It feels so good to be able to move around people without being watched too closely. Even my mother and father seem to like to move around among the noisy, milling crowd of farmers and their families mixed in with the city people. The air always has a bit of a haze from the people who smoke. That is one time that I love because everything always seems loud and fun.

We use the cutter a lot during the one and one-half to two months when our one-mile dirt road is completely snowed in. The closest blacktop county road one mile away from our house is kept plowed almost all the time. Of course, sometimes there are a couple of days in a row when even the men working the county roads can't plow fast enough to keep the roads open. A howling wind can keep the falling snow in an endless horizontal pattern with visibility only several feet. As soon as the road is cleared, it is filled in again in minutes. During so much of the winter, no matter how much I try to stay warm, whether I'm in the house or outside, I'm cold. I wonder if other kids think very much about being cold, because I sure don't hear very many complaints about the cold. There are a lot of complaints about other things. I wonder why?

In winter, sleds pulled by a teams of horses are used to take cans of milk to the Sealtest plant in Ellenburg Center for processing. My dad and George Smith take turns hauling milk to the plant from their two farms. Mostly they have a good working relationship, except when there is a milk strike.

There is no way I will be anywhere around when Mr. Smith and my father kill one of our two-hundred-pound pigs for meat. Of course, I can't help hearing my big brother Sam talking about the butchering. He doesn't seem to be bothered by much of anything. I can't figure out why Mr. Smith, with his more gentle ways, is the one that does the actual knife stick to the jugular when a hog is being butchered. My father is the one who catches the blood from the knife stick to make blood pudding. The killing and dressing of a pig is usually done in winter when there are several feet of snow on the ground. The slaughter leaves shocking pools of bright red blood staining the shimmering white snow.

Before a pig is killed, my father brings a very large kettle of water to a boil over a hearth in our one-car garage, which stands by itself a hundred feet east and on the same side of the road as the barn. There is a barrel in the garage to accept the boiling water. The killed pig is pulled up by its hind legs with a pulley and slowly let down into the barrel of boiling water so that its scraggly hairs can be scraped off. When it's lifted out of the barrel, the process continues, with the belly slit open, and then the pig is butchered.

What will be tasty hams are smoked in a metal drum in our farmhouse woodshed in front of the rows of stacked cordwood. Some of the intestines are scrubbed clean and packed with the thickened blood that will produce a deep wine-colored blood pudding. Actually, blood pudding is quite good, but it's one of the things that people big and little don't talk about. One part of the pig that seems to last forever is salt pork. The slabs are almost all fat and are about twelve inches by twelve inches and two inches thick. One side is hide. The slabs are placed among layers of salt and water in a barrel in the cellar. Months later, Ma takes a slab of salt pork out of the barrel and puts it in a bath of milk for a couple of hours then slices and fries it. The fat shrivels into small, tasteless strips. Even bread soaked in milk with a little sugar tastes better than that!

My father is a very bright man. He got a patent on a three-horse hitch. Every time somebody says something about it, I sure feel awfully proud. The patent papers are in the top middle drawer of the buffet in the dining room. There is a red ribbon with a seal on the front page. By the time my father got his patent, cars made his three-horse hitch obsolete; it was too late for him to get rich. His intelligence helps not only on our farm, but sometimes for other farmers as well. Dad forges metal in our garage to make things like horseshoes. I think it's probably what a lot of farmers do who aren't near a blacksmith's shop or somebody like my father, or if they can't get horseshoes in a store.

First my father builds a fire of wood and coal on a hearth on a bed of bricks in the back part of the garage. There are bellows overhead, which he pumps by hand to make the fire burn hotter. When the coals become red hot, Dad holds the horseshoe in the hot coals using a long-handled, scissorlike tool with his right hand while he pumps the bellows with his left hand. He holds the horseshoe in the hot coals until it starts to glow red. Next, he turns around to the anvil, a heavy iron block which is smooth on its eighteen-by-six-inch top. On one end of the anvil is a sixteen-inch-long protrusion with a rounded end that tapers from the iron block. The base of the anvil is bolted down to a wide, two-foot-high wooden tree stump. As my father turns toward the anvil, his left hand changes to the tool holding the horseshoe, and he grasps a small sledgehammer with his right hand to pound the metal into the desired shape. There are always quite a few turns from the anvil back to the fire as the metal cools and can no longer be made to change its shape until it once again is reheated to a red-hot metal.

A hay loader is the piece of farm machinery that has the smallest moving parts, and is one of the most important to have working well. A hay loader is six feet wide by ten feet high, and is pulled in back of the hay wagon. Between its two wheels are revolving teeth that pick the hay off the ground and feed it to a revolving mesh belt that carries the hay upward and dumps it into the hay wagon. It's very important to look out for things like woodchuck holes when steering a team of horses pulling the wagon and hay loader. When the wheel of a hay loader ends up in a woodchuck hole, there is a good chance that the teeth of the hay loader will get messed up because they are close to the ground in order to do a good job of picking up hay.

It is very important to let cut hay dry for only about a day or two before getting it into the barn. If it is left out too long, there is not only the threat of a possible rainstorm, after which the hay has to be re-dried, but, also, too much sun can bleach out valuable nutrition. If the hay isn't dry enough when it is stored in the hayloft, there is the threat of mold and rot, and also the threat of fire from spontaneous combustion. So, when the hay loader isn't working, my father sure has to work extra hard to try and get it repaired real fast.

My mother seems to think that my father should spend more time doing things that need to be done around the house, like repairing the broken porch windows. Of course, no wonder that Mrs. Smith's house can be so well kept. She has only one kid who is already old enough to be a teacher, and our family always seems to have a very little baby and other kids just a little bit older.

Whenever I can find an excuse to go over to the Smith's, or when I'm asked to do the Smith's Saturday house cleaning, the time always seems to go by so fast. In my mind I can pretend it's my house, with its green grass cut just so, the white of the daises, the pink of the tall hollyhocks, the prickly dark green cacti, the red geraniums, the heat of the wonderful kitchen stove in the winter. There are the fresh earth smells of spring and summer brought in by gentle breezes that ruffle the yellow curtains at the open kitchen windows, and come in through the screen of the open door from the porch with its green awning and hanging, three-person swing. It all makes me feel so good for such a little while. Every single thing is so very neat and tidy, and it's so wonderfully quiet. Maybe I'll have a house like that some day.

8

Farmland ~ Pastures ~ Rocks

Our farm is on the north side and at the foot of the Adirondack Mountains. I wonder if that's why we have rocks—big and little—everywhere. The fields that were cleared long ago to grow crops quite often have a ten-foot-across cluster of very large rocks that are surrounded by weeds, stuck in the middle. It must have been just too much for dad's family, who were on the farm before us, no matter how many horses and boy children they had, to clear the fields of stones that are so big. The smaller stones were moved to the edges of the fields to make stone walls. Most of the fields are bordered on one or two sides by stone walls with several rows of barbed wire strung on skinny wooden poles that are stuck on top of the rocks wherever there is enough space to wedge in a pole and keep it standing.

Every spring, Dad hitches up a horse to a stoneboat. A stoneboat is about five feet by ten feet and lays flat on the ground with a place in the front to hitch the horse. It's made of three-inch-thick by four-inch-wide wood slats, one grooved into the other, and there's a slight rise at the front edge. Following the stoneboat as it is pulled through the fields to pick up the fist-sized rocks the winter frost has pushed to the top of the soil is not a very nice job, so of course, no kid wants to do it. Ma's pets never seem to be the ones who end up picking rocks—kids like Rita and Rose. Marie is usually where nobody can find her. My hands get so dry and dirty because, at the most, we have only one or two pairs of gloves, and, if my big brother Sam is helping with this job, you can be sure he will be one of the ones getting gloves. Needing to pick rocks in the spring is the same for all farmers. I wonder what Mr. George Smith does with only one kid who is a teacher? He usually has a hired man.

We have three pastures on our farm. The night pasture is smaller than the day pasture and the heifers' pasture. It doesn't have trees—just scraggly grass and scrubby soil where the rocks refuse to give up enough land for crops. The cows are let out into the night pasture after the evening milking and brought back in the early morning for the morning milking.

Dad's day starts at 4:30 a.m. in the summer and a little earlier in winter so he can build fires in the furnace and in the kitchen stove. At night, before he goes to bed, he stokes the furnace in the cellar and the kitchen woodstove for the night hours. The fires burn down through the ever-increasingly bitter cold of the night. Heat to the front bedrooms on the second floor is scanty indeed. There is what is called a register in the floor of the bedrooms on the west side of the house. A metal grate approximately fourteen inches by sixteen inches is the top portion of a metal framework that opens through to the first floor. There is very little heat that comes up to the second floor through the registers.

The open stairway very near the furnace grate sends some heat up the stairs to the three bedrooms off the stairwell. By morning, the entire second floor is awfully cold. It seems to take forever for kids to get out from under warm quilts. We always put off getting up till the very last minute. For most of my brothers and sisters, every school morning means a scramble for clothes, use of the bathroom, breakfast, and finding schoolbooks. All of this looks like a disorganized mess. I guess that probably has something to do with the fact that so many of my brothers and sisters are never ready when the school bus arrives at our driveway.

I hate that one more thing the other kids can say about the Patnode kids is that they are always late for the school bus. I try to get my brothers and sisters ready to run out of the door when the bus gets to our house. I go and stand at Mom and Dad's second-floor bedroom window. The bus route passes our house going east for about a half mile before it comes back in our direction. From the window I can see it coming west from about a quarter mile away. As soon as I spy that yellow dot of a bus coming, I yell, "The bus is coming!" And the sound of my voice certainly doesn't miss too many corners of the house. "The bus is coming!"

There always seems to be at least one kid—probably Gemma—who is straggling far behind the rest. The bus driver needs the patience of a saint. Sometimes it just becomes too long a wait and the driver leaves without that last kid. No other families seem to have the problem of kids not being out at the road to get picked up by the bus. Another thing that might make a difference is that nobody else has quite as big a family as ours.

The winters seem so very long, but finally springtime arrives and the earth comes back to a new beginning of vibrant life. Most of the winter snow melts away. The well, which is a quarter mile in back of the barn and supplies both our farmhouse and the barn with water, pours out into a much wider stream than usual. The stream starts at the spring traveling north for several hundred feet toward the barn, then turns west through our little calf pasture and on through a three-foot-high-by-twelve-foot-long metal drum under a dirt road and on to the Smith's rocky night pasture. Where the stream leaves the spring, there are bright yellow flowers resting on their round fat green leaves. Buttercups and reddish orange-brown paintbrushes sprinkle the green grass in the hayfield to the east. Clusters of long-stemmed, wild, purple lilies border the stream through the calf pasture. The earth gives off the smell of its renewing life, and the powder blue sky with its puffy white clouds joins in the chorus of joyful sights and sounds of spring.

Every spring, frogs lay their eggs in the slow-moving parts of the stream. The tiny black dots in the center of each slimy egg within a cluster soon turn into pollywogs. I always gather some pollywogs that I bring home in a jar to live until they turn into frogs. I sure would turn them loose in a hurry as soon as they became frogs. I bring a jar of them into the house and change their water every day from the same stream where I got them. Their little oval bodies have a tiny tail, which makes it easier to see if they are still living. They always end up dead no matter how hard I try to keep them alive. Sometimes I sleep on a cot in the second floor middle bedroom near an open window facing the barn. Even though the barn is between the stream with the pollywogs and the bedroom window, when the pollywogs turn into frogs they sure make an awful lot of noise in the late evening and into the night. I wonder if frogs do any thinking.

The quarter mile of dirt road going south from the barn between our farm and the Smith's farm is part of the daily cow path for both our day and night pastures. There is only one gate, which is made of wood and barbed wire, to our day and night pastures. When the road turns west, the Smith land borders both sides of the road. To get to his day pasture, Mr. Smith herds his cows from his barn on the north side of the road, through his night pasture, to the wooden gate on the side of the road, then across the road and through the wooden gate on the south side.

After we milk each of our cows, we let her out into an enclosed holding area, which is in the middle of the different sections of the barn. After we have milked all the cows, we open a sliding door at the back of the barn. Somebody then follows the cows down the quarter-mile dirt road to close the barbed wire gate after the cows have gone through. On the south side of the gate is a four-hundred-foot-long-by-thirty-foot-wide path of rutty earth covered in small rocks and grass. The path ends with the night pasture to the left and the day pasture straight ahead across a small stream and up the side of our small mountain with its ever-decreasing stand of tall trees.

Scattered over the lower part of the mountain are rocks—big and little—as well as the decaying stumps of all the trees that have been cut down over the years. A little farther up on the left side is the sugar bush with the stand of tall maple trees, and past that, at the top of the mountain, is the mysterious forest. Straight ahead at the top of the mountain is the Big Rock. It is forty feet long at the bottom and reaches twelve feet into the air at its highest part. To the right there is a fence that runs east and west that separates our pasture from the Smith pasture. In this part of the pasture, there is a scanty growth of grass, moss-covered rocks, blackberry and raspberry bushes, evergreen trees, and brush that stretches over many acres.

Halfway up the mountain is where the isinglass test pit was dug. I sure wonder what life would be like if it had been a working mine. Maybe we would be rich or maybe we wouldn't have been born. After all, the hole was dug long before we came along.

On the road to the Smith's farm, and near their north-side cow gate, are the remains of a factory that we were told was used for the processing of a milk product. All that is left is the base of what were cement walls at one time, and now they are almost at ground height. There are just enough old rusted pieces of metal to help us think up all kinds of ways the place might have been used. Farm families sure don't spend much time talking about personal stuff, and probably don't think about foolish things like that.

Our third pasture—the heifer pasture—is a half mile up the LaClair road and south of our night pasture and hayfields. That is not a pasture to explore. There is only a gate to the pasture somewhere in our far-off hayfield. Farther to the south and bordering the heifers' pasture is New York State land with its never-ending mountains, streams, and forests. Stories of people getting lost—even dying—in the state land sure makes even the bravest kids never go there and pretty much stay out of the heifers' pasture. Besides, everybody knows that bears live in those parts, and what bears are like.

We use the third pasture for heifers. They are very young cows who are past the calf stage, but have not yet freshened into milking cows because they have yet to deliver their first darling little babies on wobbly legs. The heifers are herded to their pasture as soon as there is enough grass for them to eat. There is a stream that comes from the direction of the third heifer pasture then through the back hayfields and then through the night pasture. We put a salt block on a stick for the heifers in their pasture. There is a salt block on a stick for the milking cows at the back of the day pasture, and loose salt in a trough built into the wall as they come into the barn. When the heifers are first let out in the spring, the bellowing and their crashing excitement is everywhere. At last they are free from their long winter imprisonment.

At last the heifers' long summer days of freedom in their far-off pasture comes to an end. When they are herded back to the barn, they are creatures of the wild. They bolt in every direction. Whoever is helping has to run back and forth trying to keep them going toward the barn. Boy, is it cold. There will have been a light dusting of snow and the heifers, Dad, Sam, kids—all of us—end up exhaling little clouds of white.

One time, a neighbor who lived about a half mile away came to our house in Ellenburg selling meat from a closed vehicle with rear doors. The meat looked freshly butchered. There were blades of grass clinging to several of the pieces. My father and mother thought something just didn't seem right. After all, the man didn't live on a farm and didn't work at a farm job. But they did buy a couple of pieces. My father reported his suspicions.

I went with my father and a state trooper looking for some sign of ill-doing near our heifers' pasture. We came upon a very small, heavily wooded area where the flattened grasses and dark soil indicated that, indeed, an animal had been slaughtered there. It turned out to be one of the biggest and best of our heifers.

The man had a family that we knew. My father agreed that his punishment should be probation and the payment to us of the cost of the animal. I guess that's a farmer's way of doing things.

9

Teacher ~ Patnode Family

Miss Carpenter is the teacher for grades one through six in our one-room schoolhouse. She's a Protestant and she's not French like most of the kids in our school. Actually, she never told us, but we all know because she doesn't speak French and she doesn't go to the Catholic Church, even though she sometimes talks about going to church. Our family never misses mass, so we sure know about the church part. Of course, no kids ever ask about things like that. Miss Carpenter has red hair that is curly and quite long. I'm not sure why, but I don't like red hair. I still think she's quite pretty.

The school is on the dirt road that is less than a quarter mile north from our house. There is no plumbing, and for heat there is a rather large rectangular woodstove with rounded corners. The stove is about four feet high and has a door on the shorter side that swings open on hinges. The door doesn't have a little isinglass window like the smaller stove at Aunt Cora's house. That's probably a good thing, because the kids who are farm boys would probably have poked a hole in it. The stove has a place on top where Miss Carpenter can put a kettle or saucepan.

I love it so when Miss Carpenter gets rice from some government program for free and brings it to school. She cooks up a large batch and it sure disappears in a hurry. But, best of all, is when she brings her very own raisins to add to the rice. There aren't any fights among the kids about any of this. I can't imagine any other teacher cooking a batch of rice for her kids and then sometimes adding raisins she brought from home.

One of the other wonderful things that she does is help us make "jelly copies." She fills a shallow pan—about one-half inch deep—with what looks like a cloudy, firm jelly, and then something almost mysterious, but very wonderful, happens. When she presses printed paper against the jellylike stuff, enough of the image transfers to the jelly so that, when she presses plain sheets of paper down on the jelly, copies of the image appear on them. It doesn't take many pressings before we can barely make out what's on the copy.

Both my mother and father come from a family of eleven kids. My father's brother Ed is the Uncle I like to visit. His brother Bill is the snooty one married to a very big, homely woman. None of us kids is ever invited to Uncle Bill's house, which is only a mile and a half from our house. Neither he nor his wife ever speaks to any of us—even when we go into his store, which is across the street from his house. I sure wish I could talk to somebody about how bad that makes me feel, especially since I hear things about how friendly he is with a lot of other people in my father's family—like with his sister Aunt Lillian and her kids.

Actually, his being friendly with Aunt Lillian doesn't make me too jealous because I like her a lot even though her daughters—my cousins—aren't very friendly. The few times I have been able to visit her house in Plattsburgh, New York, she was so very nice. One time she gave me a beautiful white crocheted triangular head scarf edged in a beautiful pale blue green that she made. I loved it so. It made me feel so very special.

My father got the Patnode family homestead after his brothers and sisters left home. I wish I knew more about how that happened. Both my father's mother and father were dead before I was born. There is something about my father's family that we kids sometimes talk about with pride. Actually, pride is a sin, but it made me feel better thinking about it anyway. My dad's family sure had their pride. Just before they all went their separate ways, they showed the uppities—who weren't French and who were mostly Protestants who lived in the villages of Ellenburg Center, Ellenburg Corners, and Ellenburg Depot—who was really at the top by spending a lot of money on the family house and getting a big car. Maybe it wasn't true, but then maybe it was, about the family finally coming out on top. Most of the farm families are of French descent and very poor. In my grandparents' time, the family name was spelled Patenaude. I don't know why the spelling was changed to Patnode.

The Patenaude family fixed up the house with beautiful maple hardwood floors through the entire west side of the house. The first-floor rooms that have the nice floors are a small bedroom, the dining room, and the living room. This is the room that has the fireplace that sent more smoke into the room than up the chimney the few times we started a fire in it. Dad said that was because it hadn't been built right and it wasn't "drawing," whatever that means. With the smoking problem, it sure hasn't been used very much, even when thick frost with its many lacy designs covers the windows and it's bitter cold outside.

The maple hardwood floors continue from the dining room up the stairway to the second floor. There is a landing after only two steps where there is a window that looks out over our little orchard, then the stairs turn right and up about seven steps to the other two-and-one-half-foot-square landing. There's another right turn, then three more steps to the second-floor hall. There is one bedroom straight ahead. To the right, a narrow hall, with two small windows over the stairs, leads to two small bedrooms that have hardwood floors. Two of the bedrooms have their own small closets. The third bedroom, in the northwest corner of the house, has a cardboard closet next to the railing that separates the hall and the open stairway. To the left at the head of the stairs is the old part of the house with rooms that have worn linoleum on the floor.

I already told you that many years before I was born, we heard that Dad's family bought the fanciest car in all of the Ellenburgs. I think they may have gone into rather a big debt to buy the car and have the hardwood floors installed in the house, but with Dad and his brothers grown up, what better time to show that they were at the top of the social heap? At least that's what I guess. By the time my father took over the farm and paid off—what I heard only in whispers—eight thousand dollars to each of his sisters, and I never heard what amount to his brothers, I don't think my father could have had very much money left, if any at all.

After my father married my mother, they had a hired girl to help with housework and a hired man to help with barn chores. As the number of kids kept growing, and we girls got bigger, the hired girl had to go, but, of course, the hired man had to stay no matter what until Sam, my oldest brother and the first child born, was old enough and big enough to do a man's job. I think my father must have been very disappointed that, after Sam, the next five kids were all girls. I'm the fifth kid in the family. I sure help with barn chores, but girls, no matter how hard they try, just aren't as strong as boys.

My father can't do everything by himself. There are all the cows to be milked morning and night, and the cows, horses, pigs, and chickens to be fed morning and night. The manure has to be loaded and carted to the fields to be spread for fertilizer, even through snowdrifts where the manure rests on top of the snow as it is forked off the sled. Then there is planting and haying, and a lot of other stuff that has to be done.

Sometimes, at the beginning of the school year, some of us kids get our very own pencil boxes. When I get one, I love it to bits. Mine usually has only one drawer; it's not like the ultra fancy ones that have two drawers. The really showy pencil boxes have three drawers. The top part of a one-drawer pencil box has an eraser, pencils, a pen that has to be dipped in an ink bottle, and some crayons. The drawer holds a small map, and a little metal protractor for measuring angles.

What I like best of all about pencil boxes are the crayons. They have such a nice smell that sometimes I bring them up to my nose just to smell them. It's so nice to be able to make my very own pretty pictures. Miss Carpenter copies eight-by-eleven-inch sheets of paper picturing Holland's tulip fields or farm scenes for us to color. I can make them beautiful, like a never-never land, with many different colored flowers and the bluest sky. I gently touch the page with my treasured crayons using the softest yellow, the lightest pink, the brightest red, and then gray/brown for trunks of trees. Flimsy white clouds gently stray through a soft blue sky with the delicious green of the trees and grass giving a so-special life to my treasure. I make such pretty pictures that, whenever Miss Carpenter treats us with her magic jelly pictures, mine is one of the ones put up on the bulletin board. She doesn't use her copy pan just for pictures for us to color. Sometimes she copies a school assignment or other school stuff, which certainly isn't as much fun.

10

Moon Pond

Moon Pond is a big, mysterious pond that is way back in the woods. Even before we were old enough to go to school, we kids were always warned not to go there. Back then we spoke only French. Our mother and father are as strict about us speaking only in French as they can be, but it gets harder and harder as each kid—a new one almost every year—goes off to the one-room schoolhouse where the teacher speaks only English. In fact, Miss Carpenter doesn't even know how to speak French. Of course, that leads to us whispering secrets in French, which causes her to give us dirty looks and tell us, "Speak English while you're in school."

I heard so much about Moon Pond that I thought about going, but I couldn't go by myself. I didn't even know where to find it. What I did know was that, if I went about one mile east on the dirt road in front of our house, then turned north into another farmer's land, I had a good chance of bumping into Moon Pond. Another thing to worry about was that there might be a bull in the pasture around the lake, and everybody knows that bulls are dangerous. Daredevils like my brother Sam, who sneaked off to the pond, spoke of their adventures only in whispers.

I just knew it had to be wonderful because the whispers disclosed the secret that there is a place in the middle—God knows how big a place—where the pond is deep enough to be over my head. I had never been in water any deeper than a few inches. Then it happened. Somebody drowned in my Moon Pond. Even when more things came out about the drowning, I still wanted to go. Several troopers had taken a small boat out on the pond looking for the body. After that, the voices telling the story trailed off, and I couldn't make out anymore words.

I needed some help to get to the big pond. My oldest brother Sam could be depended upon if I was trying to get in trouble. He is mean to me a lot of the time. He has chased me with a snake more than once. When he is milking a cow, if I am close enough, he squirts me with milk. Sometimes he is even meaner—like hitting me. But, boy, is he good if I want to do something that might get me into trouble.

I managed to hide a blue bathing suit from my mother, who thinks there is something sinful about too much leg or peeking boobies showing. There doesn't have to be much showing in order for her to decide that a garment falls into the sin category, and I didn't want to take any chances. The bathing suit came from one of the huge wooden boxes of clothing from my Aunt Clarinda's church.

All the clothes from Aunt Clarinda smell of mothballs. I did wear one coat, even though it made me very uncomfortable because it certainly didn't look as if it was store bought for me. We were making a family trip to the Gagnier family in Chairbusco, New York. They are the family's rich relatives. My grandmother's sister married into that uppity family, and now she is one of the gang who only puts up with our large carload of parents and kids about every five years or so when she has to. After all, she can't ask someone not to come if a family member has died—at least not if that family member is a pretty close relative.

I'll never forget that day. All the high-class relatives showed up in clothes I just knew had been bought especially for them. I was wearing a grass green coat that was a little too small and a little too short. The coat had a very big rusty red fox collar and smelled of mothballs. My family doesn't have money for luxuries like bobby pins, and I hadn't yet learned from my Buffalo cousins about using socks to put up my hair to make curls. There I was with the green coat, straight brown hair, spaces where my two front teeth used to be, and metal-rimmed glasses.

I've already mentioned my two missing teeth, and how I don't smile very much. Sometimes when we kids get gum, which isn't very often, I stand in front of a mirror with the extra space covered with gum and I smile thinking about how wonderful it would be to have teeth like everybody else. On top of that, if I didn't have to wear glasses and had curly hair, I think I would be quite pretty.

Back to the Gagniers' house. Everything looks so perfect. There are flowers and candles on the dining room table. The china closet is filled with all kinds of beautiful dishes. There are no marks or scratches on the polished furniture, and no dirt or worn places on the sofa and chairs in the living room. Curtains hang in all the windows. We sure don't get to stay very long in the house.

There are huge storage barns at the back and to the west of the house that resemble Quonset huts, only they are much bigger. The barns hold a very large potato harvest. Something else that is whispered about is that, under the potatoes, liquor is stored that the Gagniers bootleg from Canada. To think they have such airs around us because we are a poor and a big farm family with horses, cows, pigs, and chickens.

Finally I was getting ready for my trip to Moon Pond. I took out of hiding the shiny blue bathing suit that came from the Buffalo box. it is a held-together affair with stringlike straps that ties in the back of the neck. The top is a puckered material joined to a plain satin bottom that is formed into a slightly flared short skirt. Of course, I couldn't let any of my growing boobs show, and I sure wasn't accustomed to having so much of my legs show, so I ended up constantly tugging at the hemline. I wore the forbidden bathing suit under a dress until we got to the pond—the same way I wear a forbidden black sweater to school that came from the same box.

Boy, was this going to be fun! Sam was up to it. How we ever got to the pond and back home again without a huge mess, like Ma finding out, I don't know. The only thing I can think of is that it must have been a Sunday when we went to different masses. The church, St. Edmund's in Ellenburg Corners, is four miles away, so getting all of us into our Sunday best and to church is hard. Almost anything could be going on—a bath, looking for clothes, getting dressed, caring for a younger kid, eating, searching for something, or a last hidden elbow to another kid's ribs which might be payback or just because somebody felt like it. Finally there is everybody scurrying about in a frenzied last-minute rush with the words "Get in the car. We're going to be late!" adding to the confusion.

Well, at last Sam and I were on our way to Moon Pond. I could hardly wait to get there. The pond was hard to reach. First we walked east down the road past the Millers' farm on the north side of the road. Past the farm, we turned north into thick woods. I'm not very good at remembering the way back when I'm in someone else's woods, especially if I have never been there before, so I followed close on Sam's heels. As we came out into a clearing, there it was, the Moon Pond of my dreams, rimmed in its frame of tall green trees with the lingering musty smell of damp earth that doesn't see much sun. I told myself I wasn't scared, but that pond sure looked awfully big—especially since I don't know how to swim. I knew it was over my head in places and that somebody had died there not very long before.

One time Sam and some of us kids dammed up the little stream that runs through our night and day pastures as it splashes over small rocks on its way going north. We secured several wooden planks across the stream. It took a long time because it was something else that we weren't supposed to be doing. We would say we were going fishing or berry picking, then go to our pitiful attempt at making the water deep enough to paddle in, but the deepest we were able to manage was about one and one-half feet.

By then, the water had spread out on both sides of the stream and into the dense, seven-foot brush making a slushy muck that left the cows' legs mud covered. Their hooves made slurpy noises as they lifted their legs from one step to the next. Even our neighbor, quiet, tobacco-chewing Mr. Smith, said something about this. Our tiny little dam had backed up enough water so that, down the stream on his land, there was only a puny trickle that didn't provide enough fresh water for his cows. When George Smith told my father what he suspected we might have done, we sure had to raise the boards in a hurry.

I was scared to go any farther than waist deep into Moon Pond. It was a beautiful spot with green trees encircling the shimmering water, even though its shimmer reflected as many brown tones as blue and green ones. I soon moved from my brief waist-high exploring of its water back to the safety of the muddy bank. I never dared to go back, and I couldn't tell anybody I had been to Moon Pond, and Sam doesn't tattletale about things he is part of that we shouldn't be doing.

At last my Moon Pond was more than just a dream.

11

The Barn ~ Ned the Horse

The barn is a wonderful place for me because I love animals so much. There are cows, horses, chickens, and pigs, and each one has a different personality.

There are snotty city kids who think they're better than we are just because they don't have to get up very early like the farm boys do to help milk and feed the cows, and they never smell a little of the barn when they go to school. Actually, they aren't even city kids—they're just from one of the little villages such as Ellenburg Center, Ellenburg Corners, or Ellenburg Depot. There isn't even one of those villages somebody could really brag about—just because each one has a store and a few other buildings besides some houses.

Sometimes one of us girls will be awakened to help with the morning chores. Sure, Rose is a much harder kid to wake up, but she isn't sickly, so I shouldn't be asked to get up for milking any more often than she is. I'm a very light sleeper, so, when I hear my father's steps coming down the hall, I don't stir a muscle because I probably will be asked every time if Dad thinks I am already awake. Rose doesn't have to pretend. Anybody can tell she really is asleep. I probably should give her a good push when I first hear Dad coming down the hall so maybe she will wake up and he will ask her more often. I wonder if that would work.

Cutting and bringing in the hay as well as threshing the oats are awfully important. If the barn isn't chock-full of winter food for the cows and the other animals by fall, we will run short before spring and that sure will add to the misery of the small winter milk check if we have to try and buy hay before spring. Even when summer grass is the main food for the cows and horses, Dad feeds store-bought grain mixtures from the GLF to the milking cows to keep them healthy as well as to try to help them give more milk. What mooing and rattling of their stanchions the cows do when they hear Dad pushing the wheeled grain bin down the cement pathway in front of them. In winter, Dad feeds the cows the GLF mixture before the milking, and he feeds hay after the milking. In summer, it's the grain before the milking then, after the milking, the cows are sent to pasture.

The front of the barn faces north. It has three sections and is about twenty feet from the dirt road. Facing the barn, on the right and left, are the very old, gray, beat-up, two-story parts with gabled roofs. Those ends and the part of the barn in the back are the original barn from a very long time ago. In later years, the section in the middle with its gray tin gambrel roof was added. It joins the two front ends. The bottom part is where there are cows, heifers, calves, horses, and of course, that one big, ugly bull with a ring through his nose. The top part is a hay-loft. In the summer, sometimes chickens—usually Rhode Island Reds—wander in from the henhouse, which is in the east end of the barn, to the cement walk-way in back of the cows. Actually, that isn't too good because chickens don't care where they poop, and that's where people walk.

Our house is some two hundred feet north of the barn and on the other side of the road from the barn. In winter, with a lot of people traipsing back and forth between the house and the barn, the path turns into hard-packed snow that makes crunchy squeaky sounds when we walk on it. The path slowly keeps get-ting higher and higher. When it gets high enough, kids have to try and stay on the hard-packed middle part because, if we step off the hard crunchy part, the soft snow might very well go over our overshoes. Even that little trip outside with a biting wind sure isn't much fun.

In the middle part of the barn just inside from the milk house, there is a row of hooks on the wall on the left side. There people can hang stuff like heavy jack-ets. The animals keep the middle part of the barn pretty warm compared to out-side. My father tries to keep the back end of the middle section of the barn a little warmer. Past where the milking cows are in their metal stanchions, there is a space where the littlest calves are spread out, tied to old stanchions on rather short chains. In that section of the barn, when the bitter cold of the north wind starts making brown icicles hanging from the ceiling, it is time for my father to start another of his winter projects.

Dad uses twine to bind together the burlap bags the GLF grains come in, and he somehow makes a big burlap curtain to close off the far end of the barn where the calves are. Whatever calves are back there have to be kind of squished up near the horses on the other end. There is a seven-foot-wide cement path the entire length of this middle part of the barn. The cows' tail ends on both sides all face the cement middle, which makes milking easier. In the first two and one-half feet of cement in front of the cows is a trough where their grain is thrown and another three and one-half feet of cement for getting hay and grain to them. At each end of the middle part of the barn is a large door that opens out to the carriage sections.

Next to the coat hooks on the same side is a very large spigot where we fill water buckets. The littler kids hang the bucket over the spout to fill it and then struggle to lift it off when it's full. There is a very big stream of water when the spigot is opened up all the way. Under the spigot, the cement is slanted to a hole in the floor. One time, a tiny, fluffy, yellow baby chick managed to get into trouble by falling down the hole. I felt so awful at the sound of the panicky chirp of a chick that I couldn't even see. It took some tears and coaxing to get my father to work at getting what had been that beautiful little ball of yellow fluff out of the hole in the cement. He finally did it. Its fluff was wet and flat. It was so scared. I was so happy. I think that maybe I am Dad's favorite, because every once in a while I can get him to do things like that.

Lots of times it seems to me that farmers should be nicer to their animals. When cows freshen and they are being milked for the first time, they are usually quite nervous and sometimes kick. Some men, like my brother Sam, hit the cows very hard. When I'm around and that happens I scream for him to stop. I tell him that I will milk the cow. It takes a lot of petting and soft words to get the cow quieted down, and even then there probably will be a cow foot in the milk bucket at least once.

Another example of cruelty to the animals in the winter is when the men hit the horses really hard when they are trying to get the team to pull hard enough to move the huge two-runner sled with many logs tied to the top—or when the horses are trying to lunge through huge, deep snowdrifts.

Something that can't be helped is when the horses are tied to a sled coming down the mountain. My father has to keep the reins very tight and the back legs of the horses who are working at holding the sled back are hit by the very traces they are harnessed to. The horses have to be very strong to hold back a big sled on the mountain—or to pull out a sled that has gotten stuck in an icy stream.

Every kid wants to be liked and to be Mom and Dad's favorite. I think it is probably much harder in Catholic French Canadian farmer families to have good things happening like hugging and kissing and saying nice things to each other. After all, what possible time can farmers find for storytelling, playing ball, and things like that when there is all the hard work that has to be done in winter from before the sun comes up to long after the sun goes down? In summer, at least, with more daylight, it's more cheerful. But then, of course, just as important as farm chores are prayers. Never mind what happens here on earth, like being happy or sad. Everybody is going to be in the next world forever. That sure makes life very hard for everybody—no matter how many times they are reminded that everything counts either to get straight up to heaven or to purgatory or down to hell.

I think that the most likely for me is purgatory. Who's good enough to go straight to heaven? But, even for purgatory I sure have to watch my p's and q's. In the next world, purgatory is where all the people who still have leftover sins go—like not having told all their sins in confession. To land in purgatory, people can't have leftover sins that are too big. If the sins are really big, people face the jaws of flaming hell. Everywhere—even in places people would never expect—the devil is waiting to try and coax people to be bad. He is trying so hard to get everybody into his hell. I wonder why? My parents say the devil is stronger than the angels, so you can imagine how hard we have to work to try and make sure we don't do or think anything bad. This is very important. Just think about how hard the devil is trying to make people bad and how long they are going to be in the next world—forever!

Another big worry I have is how very important it is that I am in a state of grace when I die. Imagine if I die and I haven't been to confession to get rid of at least my mortal sins! I would go straight to hell. One thing we're told about this seems pretty funny, but I sure wouldn't want to depend on it: when very bad people, who are just loaded with all kinds of mortal sins, make a confession just before they die, God forgives them and they are able to go right to purgatory or heaven. In a pinch, they don't even need the absolution of a real priest—they just have to be really sorry in their hearts for all those bad things. It just doesn't seem fair.

Back to the barn. On the wall past the clothes hooks and the water spigot is where the horses' harnesses, collars, and bridles are hung. Across from the harnesses are the two horse stalls. The horses' behinds face the cement walkway, but the horses have more room than the cows. Each stall has a partial window, a water bucket, and ties at the far end. When we walk past a stall where a horse like Ned, who has powerful back legs, stands so close to where we walk, we sure stay out of kicking range. Ned is the closest to the double door that goes to the carriage shed with its straw-filled second floor.

A couple of years before we got Ned, a man had started a business where farmers could buy or sell a horse. I'm not sure if this is true, but I managed to just be close enough to one door or another to hear some of what the big people were saying. They thought that something very sneaky was going on—that the man gave traded-in old plow horses something to make them livelier, and he gave the wild horses something to calm them down.

Well, it was time for our old horse Tom to go. He had worked hard for a lot of years, but whether it was for the overloaded hay wagon with the hay loader hitched to the back of it, or the sled with its logs coming down the mountain and getting stuck in the little stream, Dad just had to have two horses that were going to be able to pull real hard. One strong horse and one weaker one meant that the wagon or sled would be jerked back and forth because the strong horse would pull ahead of the old horse as they both tried so hard to move the wagon or sled. There sure was a lot of hollering and hitting when that happened.

Tom went and Ned came back from that buying and selling place. I think the part about buying Ned was my brother's idea. Ned is the wildest and most beautiful horse I have ever seen. He has a black mane, tail, and fetlocks. His black coloring is framed in a cream color, and the rest is chestnut—a glossy shining coat of reddish brown. I so love this huge, beautiful horse with his never-ending prance and his blazing eyes. But I'm a little scared of him too.

Once my father and brother got Ned home, my father became convinced that Ned hadn't been broken to harness. A challenge like Ned to a farm boy like my brother Sam was irresistible. Dad thought we should try to exchange Ned for another horse, but Sam didn't want to. Ned and Sam started a little war and Sam, of course, was just as determined as Ned was to win. The battle raged on—Sam throwing buckets, Ned throwing back leg kicks. It was kind of a wonder that Sam didn't get killed. My father had forbidden me to go into Ned's stall, but I was sure that, no matter how wild an animal is, there is always a way that, with a little time, I could make it be my friend. This huge, wild horse sure scared me to bits. If a big horse was considered dangerous and a parent told us not to go near it, we kids who weren't sissies would sure have to try.

Nobody was around, and I needed a horse to get the cows for the night milking. The smaller gray horse Kit I usually use was in her stall, but Ned was going to be the horse. His huge hindquarters almost filled the whole back of the stall, and I had to get past them with the bridle. He wore a halter that was used to tie him at the head of the stall, and somehow I had to get that off and his bridle on so I could steer him. I started talking softly. He turned his head around to look at me as I came into his stall. He sure was jittery, and I had already seen what those hind legs could do when Sam was being mean. I was so scared.

I reached over and touched him as I slowly moved into the stall. I kept talking, touching him, and moving toward his head as he jerked around. Finally, I was standing near his head when he suddenly reached over and bit my arm. It didn't really hurt—well, only a little. He did leave a bite mark, but I guess he was telling me who was boss. Even though I was so scared that I could barely move, I somehow got the halter off and the bridle on. Then the trick was, after I backed him out of his stall, to get him next to something I could stand on, while holding the steering rein, so I'd be high enough to get on his back.

First, I'll tell you more about the part of the pasture where I rode Ned. At the top of our little mountain, is the very biggest rock on our whole farm—Big Rock. It is mostly covered with moss. There are scrub trees and brush all around Big Rock. Past the brush on the east side is a rather large clearing of low-growth, scraggly grass, a few mostly decayed wooden stumps, and rocks of different sizes. A little farther east is the edge of the mysterious forest. It is a terrible place to ride a horse. It is difficult to find a path through the trees, and then you have to make sure the little trunks and low hanging branches don't brush you off the horse. Thank goodness the cows almost never go into the mysterious forest. I suppose that is because there is almost nothing in there for them to eat.

Once in a while, a freshening cow disappears into the mysterious forest when it's time for her to have her calf, if it comes early and we haven't yet confined her to the barn. Cows that almost always quietly follow one another back to the barn and almost never make any kind of a fuss become wild animals when they calve in the forest. They seem to be able to find the very best hiding places to have their calves. When a pregnant cow doesn't come back with the rest of the cows, farmers know that they probably are in the farthest reaches of the day pasture. I guess the cows know that the rather barren night pasture is not a good place to hide when having a calf. With three or four men and kids spread out hunting we finally find the mother, who then starts bellowing and running. The tiny, darling, new calf with its umbilical cord hanging, is already able to run faster then we can, and tries to follow its mother. When finally we corner the calf, we have to carry it back to the barn, and the mother follows behind.

Now, back to my first ride on Ned. I think he really learned to trust me. I rode Ned bareback into the clearing next to the mysterious forest. I was looking for another horse to bring back to the barn. I had the second bridle with its lead line over my shoulder. Somehow, I had let the lead line of the second bridle fall to the ground. It got hooked onto a small bush and was pulling me to the ground. Of course, without even thinking I hung on to Ned's reins. I was dragged halfway down Ned's side when I finally let go. His huge back hooves went flying over me, and that wonderful, beautiful, outrageous horse stopped about twenty feet away and let me walk back to him. I found a stump and he stood still long enough for me to get back up. I wasn't scared any more. He knows about me. I love him so.

Year 1924
My Parents' Wedding Picture

Dad   Mom
Samuel Patnode (42 years old), Jeannette Patnode (24 years old)

Jeannette and Sam Patnode

1922

Grandmother and Grandfather Paul and Augusta Langevin
are sitting on the bumper; Uncle Roderick Langevin is
in the car.

1925

Aunt Pauline Langevin (later known as Sister Angela)
on the rake, Aunt Mina's husband Floyd Warner, and
Grandfather Paul Langevin are on top of the hay wagon.

Grandmother Augusta Langevin
feeds the chickens.

Grandmother and
Grandfather Langevin
hold their first grandson
LaVerne Warner.

Theresa's Grandmother Augusta Langevin and her mother Jeannette Patnode pose in their customary cotton dresses and aprons.

The local mailman Fred Carpenter was the father of the teacher in the one-room schoolhouse, Miss Helen Carpenter.

Fred Carpenter seated on the fender of his car waiting for mail. He delivered mail on the Star Route from the Center to Ellenburg Depot.

Grandmother Augusta Ann Langevin sits on the porch working on a knitting project.

This is the iron bridge located near where Grandmother Langevin lived.

Bridge crossing North Branch of Great Chazy River in Ellenburg Corners early 1900s.

Four of Theresa's aunts, all daughters of
Grandmother and Grandfather Langevin,
became Benedictine nuns at Saint Marys,
Pennsylvania.

Left to Right

Sister Bonaventure
Sister Angela
Grandmother Langevin
Sister Jean Marie
Sister Paula
Grandfather Langevin

Left to Right

Grandmother
    Langevin
Sister Paula
Cousin Linda
    Langevin
Sister Kathleen

about 1930

Augusta - Paul Langevin

Grandmother
and
Grandfather

Augusta and
Paul Langevin

Jan 2, 1946

Aunt Clarinda
McQuade
Aunt Sister
Jean Marie
Grandmother
Langevin
Aunt Sister
Paula

Clarinda   Jean M.   Mama   Sr. Paula

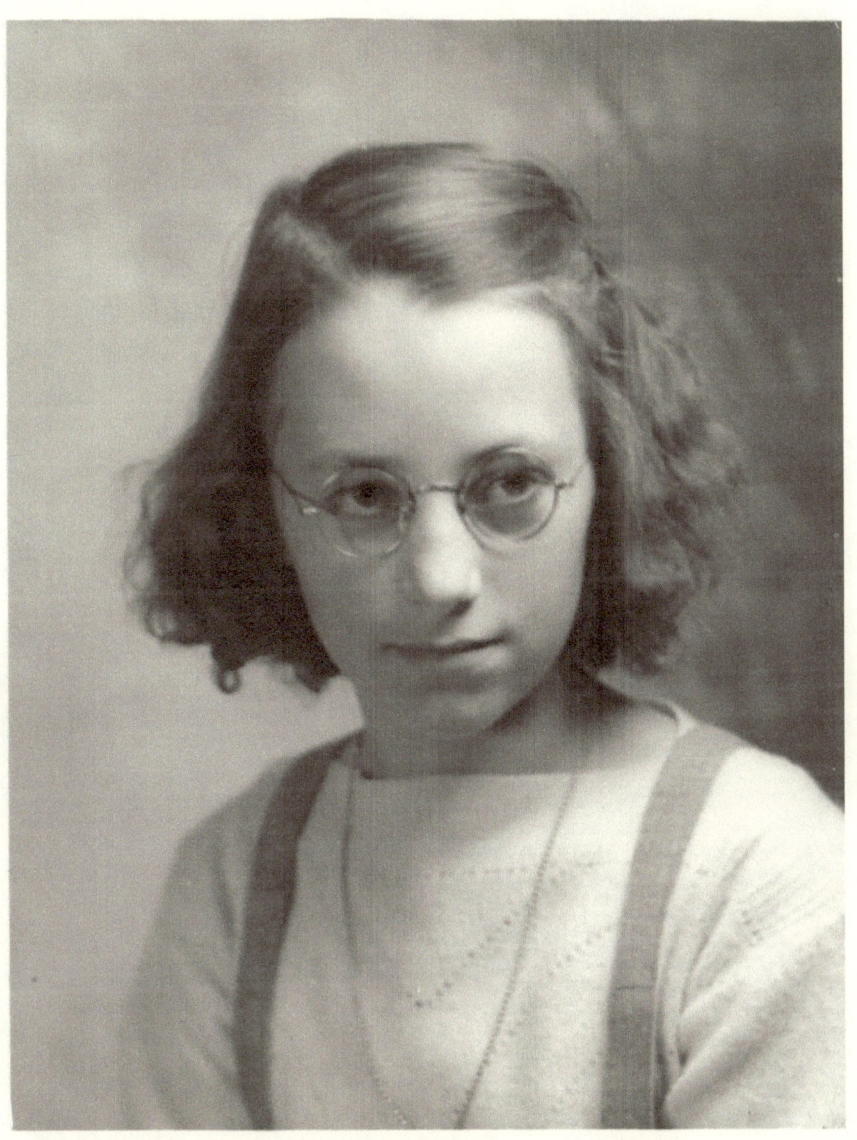

Theresa Patnode—Grade School

Theresa helps baby Bernadette get a ride on Queen.

Horse Queen   Bernie   Theresa

Theresa
Raymond   Paul Bernadette
Kit (Horse)

Theresa takes her brothers and sister for a ride on Kit. In the background to the right is the east end of the Ellenburg Center barn of the family homestead.

Theresa Patnode and her siblings attended this one-room schoolhouse for grades one through six.

1 room schoolhouse Ellenburg Center, N.Y.

Sam

Rita

Marie

Rose

Theresa

Gemma

The six oldest Patnode kids are dressed for winter snow.

The one-room
schoolhouse can just
be seen over the
snowbanks along the
north-south road
next to the Ellenburg
homestead.

Ice covers the tree branches in front of the Ellenburg Center
farmhouse, which is protected from winter cold and snow by
storm windows.

Sam Patnode with Visiting Relatives

Grandma

Dad   Uncle   Sam Jr.
Rita   Grandpa   Joe   Uncle Paul Aunt Clarinda
        Langevin   Raymond Rose
             Gemma   Theresa
   Marguerite   Paul   Jeannette

Ros. 49

Rose Marie Sam Rita
Joe Gemma Theresa

Northern Adirondack Central School
Ellenburg, N.Y.

Dr. John W. Harrold
District Superintendent of Schools
Clinton County, New York.

The gentle horse pulling small wagon with kids.

Rita
Joe   Jeannette
    Gemma   Rose   Bernadette
            Marguerite   Theresa
    Paul

Lots of Kids

Rita Dad   Martha Lisa Rose Sam
Marg Gemma   Bernie   Ray Paul Joe
            Jeannette
        Marie - missing

Summer of 1938

ali hit junin

Theresa Joe Rita

Rose Jeannette Ray

Marie Mary Gemma

Sam and Jeanette Patnode's children pose by the swing
set. The hired man's house is in the background.

The McQuade relatives from Buffalo visit with the
Patnode family.

12

Garage ~ Hired Man's House

"The hired man's house" is what we kids call it. A long time ago, I remember a hired man and his family who lived in it, but mostly it sat there with nobody—not a single soul—living in the house until my father let an awful old man and his two daughters move in. Dad built the house himself. It is across the road from our one-car garage that almost never has a car in it. But that garage sure comes in handy for a lot of other things—like butchering pigs and blacksmithing.

As you enter the garage, on the left, running the whole length of the garage, is a two-foot-wide shelf on legs. There sure is a lot of stuff on top of the shelf, over the shelf, and under the shelf as well as lots of hanging saws of different kinds.

There are hammers—a regular one for nails and a big sledgehammer with a bricklike head on a long handle. The sledgehammer is especially good for splitting up wooden chunks into smaller pieces. First, my dad uses an ax with a sharp, two-sided blade on a wooden handle to make a first cut in the chunk of wood. Next, he hammers the pointed end of a triangle shaped piece of metal called a wedge into the cut, and then hammers the wedge into the cut with the sledgehammer until the wood splits.

The long logs that are hauled down from the forest must be cut into eighteen-inch chunks that will fit into the kitchen stove and the furnace. My father uses a long, wooden, tablelike affair with a very dangerous two-and-one-half-foot-wide circular saw on one end. He fixed an old motor to turn the saw. Even brave kids know not to stand near that blade. One awful day, my father was cutting logs and somehow got his index finger too close to the whirling teeth of the saw. He was bleeding so badly. We were all so scared. Did this mean we wouldn't have anybody to take care of us—to work the farm or to keep us together? Farmers don't go to a doctor very often, but that sure was one time that Dad did. He ended up with a scarred, crooked, stiff finger, but at least he can still use his hand for things like milking, holding a pitchfork, and all the other chores.

The garage is pretty much of a mess, and it smells of old, used oil, but it isn't too bad. There are old empty oil cans that hold nails, screws, and washers. There are full cans of oil, some with spouts. There are harnesses in need of repair, a couple of old tires, and all kinds of junky stuff among the good stuff. There is a big, two-sided door on the north side of the garage by the road. There are two windows on each of the other three sides and, even though the windows are never washed, the smoky light drifting through makes the garage kind of a nice place.

When I am in the garage with my father while he is doing one of the repairs on the machinery or working with metal on the anvil, not only is he fun to watch, but he never hollers at me. I don't know why, but my father never seems to get angry with me, but Ma sure does. That is mostly Rita's fault. She is such a tattletale. She comes back with stories about what she calls my flirting with boys and other things. All I have to do is talk to a boy, and I get reported. When other people, like my mother or brothers and sisters, hear about anything like that, the teasing is loud and long and not very nice. They say things like I'm boy crazy. Rita is also likely to report if I am one of the two kids sent to get water for school and we take too long. After all, who knows what we might have been doing? I don't think it's really teasing—it's just people being very mean and it makes me feel awful. I sure know to try and hide any kind of flirting or anything else that might lead to what my mother and the other kids call teasing.

One time, the hay wagon, with its team of horses, was out in front of our house. There wasn't any hay in the wagon. From as long as I can remember, we kids always have loved to ride on that wagon—with or without hay. I was only three or four years old. A big hired man was on that wagon, and for once there wasn't anybody else around. Why he was there with the wagon I don't know—probably to get my brother Sam or my dad. But he tried to coax me to go for a ride to the field in the back of the house. I stood there wanting to go for that ride, but there was just something funny about how he was looking at me. I stood there for a minute or two next to the house's steps then turned and went back into the house. I'm not very old now, but I can remember that.

My father made a pretty nice little house when he built the hired man's house. One of the two entrances into the house is through the woodshed door. Often, where I live, houses are built with woodsheds off the kitchen entrance to the house. All the rooms are quite small. The kitchen has a window on the south side. On the west wall on the left is a kitchen cabinet, then a door leading to the living room, a bit of wall, then another door to a small bedroom. On the north wall is a door to the bathroom with its sink, toilet, and tub.

The living room has a door that leads to a small, enclosed porch on the front of the house. On the opposite wall of the living room is an archway that opens to another small room and an open stairway that leads to the second floor. On that same side of the room, next to the stairs, is a stove that works the same way as a potbellied stove, but it is shaped like a cube, with a hinged door on the side and small black legs underneath. On the second floor, at the top of the stairs, is a hall that runs the whole length of the front of the house except for a rather large closet at the far end. The second floor has slanted ceilings with two little bedrooms on the north side.

For many years, when Dad hired men who were the sons of nearby farmers, the house stood empty. So my dreams, when they aren't filled with terror of big snakes—especially when Sam has just chased me with a snake or been mean to me—are of living alone in the hired man's house.

If I lived in the hired man's house, I'm sure it would be so very peaceful. First of all, it would be quiet—no fighting words, no screaming, no crying babies ... just the sounds of the wind and the rain, the sounds of the forest. The murmuring brook, the doves' coos, the grasshoppers' chirps, even the sound of thunder off in the distance, all would have such peace for my soul. Here I am, fifth in a family still growing. The only time that everybody—well, at least the girls and Ma—seem to all enjoy something is the one time a year in the spring when we go for a picnic in the woods. It usually is a little chilly. We take blankets, sandwiches of homemade bread with peanut butter, and apples if there are any left from the winter storage.

It seems to take forever, but at last springtime arrives. Not only are the leaves on the trees starting to open, but everything is beginning to stir. Best of all, soon I will mostly be free from the house. There will be horseback rides to get the cows for evening milking, berries to pick, a garden to plant, apples and crab apples in trees, tame cherries next to the woodshed, and wild cherries along the north stone wall, not to mention the flowers—roses, hollyhocks, morning glories, and lilies. There are the scarce, beautiful, little purple violets with their fragile, tiny petals. Ma will be so happy if somebody finds one to bring back to her—at least I think she will. They usually make her smile. We sure try hard to be the kid to bring that treasure back to her. The once-a-year picnic—if only there was some way to make it last longer and to have other family fun times.

Well, actually, once in a while, there are some fun things squashed in, even if there is a lot of sadness most of the time. For example, sometimes there is skating when the snowdrifts start to melt in the spring. If the warming weather is just right, we might have as many as three places to skate, although the one in back of the house is always the best. There is a gentle slope down from all sides to form a tiny valley about one eighth of a mile long and about two hundred feet wide, narrowing at both ends. The one in the front of the house is only the size of our rather big yard. The one in back of the barn comes from the spring, so, because there is not only melting snow but running water, we can't depend on what the ice will be like unless somehow the melting snow has formed ice about thirty feet across almost all the way to the LaClair road.

There is always a scramble. Here we are, a lot of kids and only one pair of skates—my mother's old black leather shoe skates. The only other things we can use for skating are metal runners that fasten to the soles of our shoes with little tabs that are tightened to fit with a key. The runners can never be made tight enough not to wobble. It's not very nice when I get up a little speed and the back or front of my runners become loose. No wonder I'm so good at falling—I've had a lot of practice between all the skating falls and all the times I've fallen off a horse.

I stopped counting the times I fell off horses when I got to ten. I keep dreaming about having a saddle so I'd have something to hang on to if a branch tries to brush me off a horse's back or I lose my balance on a trotting or galloping horse. Of course, if I fall off a horse I have to get right back on. Only sissies don't get right back on a horse after they fall off. Boy, when I am the one who gets Ma's skates, I stuff the toes with newspaper and wear two pairs of socks to make them fit, then I sure have fun. I think, if I had my own skates, I could become a good skater. With all us kids, and the ice not lasting very long, and all the chores to do, there isn't much skating that happens. During the few times I manage to be the first one to get to Ma's skates, I'm pretty shaky to start. What a feeling to go skating into the biting-cold, crisp air!

That awful man with his two daughters had moved into the hired man's house. I don't know where he came from or if he even ended up paying us any money, but there was something very bad—almost evil—about him. There he was in my dream house. I don't know how, but Ma knew and wanted to get rid of him much sooner than my father did. My father didn't seem to do much of anything about certain things.

One of the things my father did made me so sad. He took his gun off the top shelf in the washroom and went out to kill a dog that belonged to Uncle Bill. I don't know how he knew it was Uncle Bill's, but he seemed to know. Both my mother and father dislike dogs, and we had seen this dog quite a few times on our property in back of the barn. The dog hadn't been caught doing anything bad. Ma told my dad not to kill the dog because it was Uncle Bill's. When Dad took the gun down and I heard what he was going to do, I ran upstairs to the mothball closet, closed the door, and covered my ears. I came out quite a bit later. My father was a pretty good shot and, even though the dog was a few hundred feet away, he had managed to hit it. When I came down from the closet, it had crawled all bloody to the front porch. Just then, even though I didn't want to—not even for a minute—I hated my father. Of course, that didn't last too long. After all, I am his favorite.

That man in the hired man's house was strange. Some of things going on didn't seem right. I heard it whispered that he took sunbaths without any clothes on up the hill in our woods. Then there was certainly a very strange thing that happened. My father, one of my brothers, myself, one of my sisters, that man, and one of his daughters were in our very big car that even had extra little seats that folded down from the back of the front seat.

There is a doctor who has an office in Ellenburg Center. The man asked my father to stop at the doctor's office. When my father stopped the car, the man turned to his daughter and ordered her out of the car with him. She looked startled and asked why. He shut her up in a hurry and again ordered her out of the car. We all waited in the car while they went inside. They both came out after quite a while. The girl was crying. What could possibly have made her cry? I just knew it was her father's fault, whatever had made her cry.

It seemed to take forever, and a lot of my mother's scolding before my father finally made the man move out of the hired man's house. Nobody else ever lived in that house after that.

A half mile north from our schoolhouse and on the west side of the road was the Godel farmhouse. We never visited anybody in the Godel house, but we had heard over the years of the many very beautiful quilts that were stored in the attic of the one-story house. It was a very cold winter day with snow two feet deep and snowbanks on the sides of the road so high we couldn't see over them. Off in the distance, one of the kids noticed smoke curling up from what looked like the Godel farmhouse. A few of us went running to the house as fast as we could. There weren't any big people around. Smoke was all we could see in the windows at the front and south side of the house. On the north side was the garage. We went to the back of the house through snow that was so deep that, with each step, we had to lift our legs very high to keep going. In the back of the house was a window with no smoke in back of it, so we broke the window into what turned out to be the bathroom.

We managed to tear a bathtub from its piping and somehow got it out of the window. We threw a lot of paper stuff that was on some shelves and other things into the bathtub. Even while we were doing this, all I could think of were the quilts—all the work that had gone into making them, and all the memories they had to hold. Well, there was no more for us to save in the bathroom. Teachers and other grown-ups always warn kids not to stay in a burning building because the floor above might collapse. I did so want to save the quilts. I really knew there was no way—I couldn't, no matter how much I wanted to. Looking through the living room windows I could already see glowing red flames. We went around to the front of the house, which was next to the road. There was the Godels' big boy who had just arrived from the village of Ellenburg Center about one mile away. I don't know how he found out about the fire, but there he was. By now smoke was pouring from the main part of the house into the garage. His car was in the garage.

Even though most of us farm kids have never been to a movie (the closest movie house is about eight miles away at Ellenburg Depot), we know that if a fire gets to the gas tank of a car and it catches fire, somebody close to it can get killed. The Godel young man was not going to have his treasure of a car burn up. He threw open the garage door. Smoke came pouring out. He ran to the barn across the road and found a chain. It sure was scary, but how could we not help somebody who rushed into all that smoke and then ran out coughing, carrying the other end of the chain he had just attached to his car? Somehow, all us kids and a few grown-ups who had finally arrived pulled the car out of the smoke-filled garage. His car was saved. The rest of the house, except our pitiful rescued bathroom things, was a total loss.

13

Haying and the Barn

The barn is filled with all kinds of things. The newer middle part is connected to the much older end parts of the barn, which are on the north side next to the road. The new part of the barn holds the cows, horses, heifers, and calves, and is about one hundred feet long. It is a two-story building with dusty small windows all across the front. The second-story roof starts just above the first-floor windows. The roof is covered with long, metal, twelve-inch-wide strips that arch upward about thirty-five feet, making a very large second-floor hayloft. Every once in a while, a very heavy wind manages to pry off a few of the metal roof strips. With all the other chores, it sure is very hard to find time to repair the roof.

The hayloft is where we store most of the hay. Haying is started as soon as the hay is barely high enough, as there is only one cutting because of the long, cold winters. Farmers sure have to hurry to get the cutting, raking, and hauling of hay into the barn finished, especially since, at the same time, they have all the regular chores to do. My very special job—and only mine—is raking the hay. Mostly I use the little gray mare Kit. She is a little horse compared to the other two horses, which we use as a team for the big chores like pulling hay wagons and sleds loaded with logs. I sure wish she could have a baby, but I was told that it was not possible. I don't know why, because both Ned and Tom are male horses, but kids don't ask about things like that. I'm not sure why.

Farm kids who do barn chores pretty much don't complain. It's a different story about doing things in the house, like washing dishes. In our house, dish-washing and drying often sparks a mini battle. I remember one time when I was the one who had the dish-washing chore. Gemma, my sister who doesn't say much, sure can show how mad she is about something probably better than any of the other kids. She doesn't hit like some of the others or scream or anything like that. The washed dishes were piling up in the rack to be dried. She was supposed to dry that day. The pile of dishes kept getting higher. I think she did about two dishes in a whole minute. I'm ashamed to tell about this part. I went and told Dad. He was very mean to her. I get a very sad feeling when I think about that.

To rake the hay, I put Kit's bridle, collar, and harness on and then take her out to where the rake is. The rake has two four-foot, spoked wheels. In the five feet between the wheels there is a rod from which hangs a row of three-foot curved, narrow teeth that collect the hay. My little metal seat is up over the teeth. Next to my right foot is the foot pedal that I use to raise the teeth when they are full of hay. The horse Kit is hitched between the wooden trestles in front of me. I steer her with the leather strap that stretches all the way from her bridle through a part of the harness, and all the way to my seat. She is a peppy little thing.

We usually start the haying some time in August when the weather has been good (not too much rain and not too little), the grasshoppers that like very dry weather have done almost no damage, and all the machinery is working well. The hay is mowed right after the morning chores. After the sun has dried the newly-cut hay for a few hours, Dad checks it to see if there are places in the field where the hay is too bunched up to have dried enough for raking. If he finds bunched up hay, he turns it over, and then the hay is left out a little longer for more thorough drying. Finally, Dad gives me the word that now is the time to start raking.

Raking hay makes me feel very good because I know that what I'm doing is such an important part of haying. I get Kit harnessed and hitched to the rake, then steer her to the field of cut hay. I start at the edge of the field going straight across to the other side. I work the tooth-release foot pedal up and down, then I steer back in the other direction, doing the same thing. I make very good straight rows up and down the field. I can pretty much tell how good the hay is going to be by how close I need to make the rows. Actually, I rake over the same place again after the hay loader has made its first pickup. Of course the second time the rows are much farther apart because there is less hay. The hay loader doesn't get every bit of hay the first time, and we need to store as much hay as we possibly can because we have very long winters.

For the next step, a team of horses is put in harness and hitched to the hay wagon. Then we hook a hay loader to the back of the wagon. Loading the hay on a wagon is usually a two-man job. The man in the front of the wagon steers while loading hay onto the front of the wagon. As the hay loader starts to dump hay on the wagon, the man in the back of the wagon spreads the hay to about two feet high. He then tosses the oncoming hay to the man at the front of the wagon, who not only steers the horse, but also arranges the hay at the front of the wagon. This continues until there is a heaping load of hay.

Every once in a while, if there is only one man to go on the hay wagon, I am allowed to be the person who steers the horses. One time, the horses ran away from me. At first, I pulled as hard as I possibly could on the reins, but they wouldn't slow down even a little bit. They were galloping as fast as they could with the wagon bouncing all over the place and me hanging onto the wagon. There wasn't anybody else on the hay wagon because it had been in a place where the hay loader wasn't being used. The men were in a hayfield on the other side of a little stream.

Horses are kind of crazy when they are running away. These two galloped full-steam across the field and bumped through the small stream to the other hayfield. One of the men ran toward me and managed to get on the hay wagon and grab the reins. He got the horses back down to a walk. I sure didn't want to do any more steering of horses that day. Sometimes, the hay wagon comes very close to tipping over. It can happen when a wheel hits a woodchuck hole, or when we round a corner too fast when we are rushing back to the barn as black clouds and streaks of lightning are closing in fast, promising a heavy downpour.

The smell of freshly cut hay is almost like perfume. I like to take deep breaths as the scent drifts up from the ground. When we are riding in the car, even without looking, I can tell if we are passing a field of freshly cut hay. It's those times when I can forget about the itchy part of working or playing in hay.

Getting the hay wagon through the very big door in the old western part of the barn is some trick, and certainly not one I ever tried. There is a slight incline from the road to the barn door fifteen or twenty feet away. When the hay wagon comes down the road from the fields, it is heading east, so to get into the barn, the man driving the horses has to make a sharp left turn up the incline with the hay wagon popping out on the sides and loaded very high on top. Whoever is on top of the hay wagon has to duck to avoid hitting his head on the door frame. The horses have to be moving fast to miss the sides of the barn door and to pull the heavy wagon up the incline without getting stuck. Once the wagon is inside the barn, it sure is a good feeling. If we have to go out for another load before the night chores, we sure have to hurry to unload the hay.

There are so many things to make me proud of my father. Dad used an old car motor fixed up with belts, pulleys, and ropes, to haul the hay from the wagon to different places in the hayloft. There is a metal pan under the motor to catch any oil that might spill. There is a metal track along the peak of the roof in the middle barn on which a big fork moves back and forth. The fork grabs forkfuls of hay in the wagon. The fork has two teeth about two and one-half feet long that clamp together to hold a bunch of hay.

Dad starts the motor with a hand crank that looks the same as the ones on very old cars. Next, with a rope and levers, he brings the fork all the way over to where the hay wagon is. My dad loosens the rope that holds the fork so that, with a jerking motion, he can plant the fork into whatever part of the hay wagon he is unloading. He sets the fork with a big mouthful of hay and then, using the power from the motor and pushing and pulling on a rope, he guides the fork up in the air to the metal track.

At the beginning of the haying, Dad unloads the hay in the middle of the hayloft with a special jerk of the rope, but it doesn't take much of a pile in the middle before the fork has to be lowered just right to a second man in the hayloft. The second man then heaves and pushes the hay-filled fork till he hollers out "now" (or something like that) to my father to let him know to release the hay in the fork. Then my father gives a big tug of the rope to let the hay from the fork go flying in the right direction.

There are four three-and-one-half-foot-square holes in the floor of the hayloft. We push hay down from the hayloft through these holes so it lands right in front of the cows. There are two on each end of where the milking cows are on the north side of the barn. On the south side, there is one in front of the milking cows and the other one is in back of the third horse stall in front of where the calves are chained. Near that one, there are narrow boards nailed to the wall that we can use to climb up into the hayloft and, of course, also to come down. Pushing hay through these openings in the floor is hard work for kids, and even the men and big boys breathe hard after that chore. It's especially hard in the months of March and April when the hay has gotten packed down over the winter months.

There are a lot of things for me to worry about. We aren't supposed to watch any of the goings on at the farm like calves being born. I guess that sort of thing could give kids bad thoughts of some kind or other, and such experiences would probably give the devil a chance to get at us again. Sometimes I try to peer down the holes from the hayloft, but I really can't see very far without the chance of getting caught. I so much want to see a calf being born. At our house there is a veterinarian book on the fireplace in the living room. It is one of those forbidden things, but when no one is looking, I sneak a good long look. It actually has a picture of a calf coming out of a cow. I think that is probably why it is not allowed, because I can't find anything else that is something a kid isn't supposed to see. Even the Sears Roebuck catalog gets awfully close to the forbidden because of the pictures of people in long johns, brassieres, and things like that.

If it is a good year and we fill the hayloft, we put the extra hay in the spaces where there isn't even a floor in the west part of the old barn next to where the hay wagon is kept. One time, when there wasn't any hay in that section, the calf I called my very own fell down the three feet into where there had been some hay. I was crying very loud and hugging the calf. It seemed to take forever for my father to come and help me get my calf out of there.

We store the oats in a pile in the far corner of their very own little room in the northwest corner of the same part of the old barn. That's the same room where the electricity comes into the barn from a pole on the other side of the road, and where we store bags of GLF feed. My father's rather large-wheeled grain bin, which he uses to hold the GLF feed and which he pushes in front of the cows when he is giving them grain, stands covered outside of the grain room when it's not being used. When the horses are going to be pulling hay wagons into the barn, we leave the grain bin in front of the cows.

The section of the barn where the hay wagon is brought in is two and one-half stories high. There is a very rickety ladder fastened to the north wall, which reaches to the very peak of the roof. At the very top there is a small opening through which I can see for a very long way. It sure is pretty scary to climb all the way to the top because sometimes one of the wooden slats of the ladder breaks away, and sometimes slats are missing. Willingness to climb that ladder is just another one of the things that shows whether a kid is a sissy or not. Looking out of the little opening all the way at the top is so special. I can see so very far away and dream a little bit about different things.

There is a daredevil thing that I barely got myself to do just once. Over that same pit into which the calf had fallen, my brother Sam fastened a long twelve-foot-by-twelve-inch board that we could use as a diving board into the little bit of hay that was left down below. It looked a couple of stories high, but I can't be sure. Of course, he, being a boy and seven or eight years older than the rest of us, was showing off. He kept saying I was a sissy if I didn't jump, so, I just had to do it. I was so scared. I walked slowly to the end of the board and looked down. There wasn't much hay left down there, and it sure looked an awfully long way down. I just couldn't, but I just had to—this once anyway. Finally, I jumped. I don't know why there are so few broken bones in my family.

Another time, in the same section of the barn where there is some hay stored in front of and overhead of where the hay wagon comes in, Rose and I had a secret place. We brought a sandwich and—of all things—matches to our secret place! I never told anybody, especially my family, about that one. Even very small kids know better than to do that. I sure am glad nothing bad happened.

I am only allowed to see a calf after it is born, and not while it is coming out of its mother. Sometimes they still have the umbilical cord hanging underneath and are all wet and messy looking. When Dad thinks that cows are about to have their babies, he ties the cow all the way at the far end of the cows' stalls. When I am allowed in after the calf is born, near the cow's behind will be a big, shiny, reddish blue, almost flat bag in a rather bloody mess of what, I guess, came out of the cow with the calf. At least that mess I am allowed to see, but I really want to see the real thing of a calf being born.

One time, we had twin calves. They were quite small and very precious little darlings on wobbly legs. Dad said they could be mine but then it didn't matter—they were too small to grow up to give a lot of milk, so they had to go. All farm kids know that farmers can't afford to keep calves that won't be good milkers because they will eat as much as the cows that will be good milkers.

There is only one bull on most farms, so usually all male calves as well as most of the female calves are taken away to be sold. They usually leave with the delivery of cans of milk to the factory. Calves are put in burlap bags up to their necks and tied with twine. They bleat and struggle furiously to be free. From the part of the barn where the mother cow is tied comes an awful, loud bellowing sound. Everywhere are echoes of pleading and terror. I knew my twins were going to die. I cried hard, but no matter. Dad and the other farmers have to send as much milk as possible to the milk factory. I wonder if city kids have things that make them very sad.

14

Life on a Farm

Most of the time, our bull is kept in a stall all the way at the west end of where the milking cows are. There is a three-inch metal ring through the middle part of his nose that just hangs down. Even my father and the other farmers are careful around those big brutes. Sometimes, if a bull seems awfully mean and scary—like the ones that bellow and paw the ground with one of their front hoofs—the men grab the ring with a hook that's on the end of a long stick. The bull moves when the ring is tugged to avoid pain in his tender nose.

During the summer, one of my chores is to get the cows out of the day pasture and to the barn for evening milking. I bridle up small, gray Kit and ride bareback to get them. Sometimes, it is kind of easy because the cows have already started down our little mountain toward the barn. Other times, when I count how many cows are on the path toward home, there are some missing. The cows might be in the south or the southwest area of the pasture, or even in the mysterious forest. The southwest pasture is where there are bunches of prickly blackberry bushes and not much grass. There are lots of rocks—some small and some a couple of feet across. There aren't very many maple trees, big or little. It is one of the places we go when we are looking for a Christmas tree to cut down, even though there are not very many evergreen trees anywhere on our farm.

The night pasture, which is northeast of the day pasture, has a lot more rocks; in fact, so many rocks that trees don't grow there—well, maybe three or four real little ones. The mysterious forest is the hardest place in which to find a cow because there are a lot of little trees—mostly maples—growing very close together. It is so easy to get brushed off the horse if I'm not very careful. Sometimes it seems as if Kit is trying to brush me off when she makes a little turn by herself and I have to grab on to her mane real fast or down I go. If the woods are too thick, I just get off her back and lead her where I want her to go.

Every once in a while, my father lets the bull out with the cows. It's quite scary when I have to get the cows on horseback and the bull is in with the cows. I can't help but wonder what it would be like if I fell off and the bull was close by and feeling mean. Would he come after me? There are stories that we kids hear about bulls—things like people being chased and about farmers getting killed by a bull. I think the stories are true, but I'm not sure. It is enough to see them pawing and hear their bellowing to be scared around them.

I love galloping my horse Kit, but we all know not to get cows excited by trying to make them run before they are going to be milked, so I never try to hurry the cows when I'm driving them to the barn to be milked. When the cows are a quarter mile from the barn, I wait for them to get way ahead of me, then I gallop the rest of the way back to the barn. I sure don't do that when a bull is among the cows. I ride bareback and I don't want to take any chances of falling off. It's not as if I have a saddle to hang on to if I get into trouble.

The barn is very important to me. I spend as much time as I can in the barn because it seems to me there is always screaming and fighting going on in the house. The north middle part of the barn is forty feet high with a metal gambrel roof. In the barn are the cows, heifers, calves, a bull, horses, various cats, and sometimes a dog. There is a large two-and-one-half-story section of the barn on the east end and the west end. When you look at the entire barn from our house, which is a couple of hundred feet north of the barn, the two ends of the barn look like two great big, very old two-and-one-half story houses facing the road with slanting roofs and with their sides attached to the cow part in the middle. The two ends have sides of old gray horizontal wooden slats and roofs that leak. Whenever we look up through those roofs, in quite a few places, we can see daylight. That is just another one of those things that my father is certainly too busy to fix. There always are more important things to do.

From the sky, the whole barn would be the shape of an uneven great big square with a big open space in the middle. The cows are led in from the pasture through the old back part of the barn, through the empty middle, and on to the front middle part for milking, then back out the same way. I don't understand how cows know that after the morning milking, they go to the day pasture, and after the evening milking they go to the night pasture.

The very old south middle part must have been built a whole lot of years before any of us kids was born. It is such a wonderful place to explore and, in some ways, a little scary. On the west side storage area is some old farm machinery that is falling apart and hasn't been used for many years. Sometimes hens' nests, which might be very old or quite new, are hidden under an old cracked and disintegrating leather seat or the cushion of a battered, useless, very old cutter or very old car. There are missing floor boards in the floor, and the boards that are there are shrunken. There are some boards that still hold on at one end and hang a foot or two to the ground below on the other end. Endless, uneven curtains of gray, dusty cobwebs hang from the beams overhead. The irregular, knotted beams bend under the load of the second floor, and a few pitiful shreds of bark cling to them. If I move too fast, the air quickly fills with a choking dust.

At the west end of that same south part of the barn are some rickety steps that lead up to the second floor. Just a few feet from the top of the stairs is a space where the old west part of the barn meets the even older south part of the barn. Where the two roofs meet, is a cozy place about five feet from the floor where pigeons nest. They sure make a mess with their poop. They are so pretty though. Some of them are almost all gray and some almost all white. The pigeon call—the drawn-out coo coo—seems to never stop day or night. I wonder if they are talking to each other. Their call is so different from the noise that other birds make that it's easy to tell the difference.

A bird that seems almost mysterious, and I almost never see, is the tiny, darting little hummingbird. Its wings are so very fast and it moves so quickly. Even if I see a little movement from the corner of my eye, it isn't easy to actually see the bird because, by the time I move my eyes toward it, often it's gone. Hummingbirds are never around the barns. I've only seen them on the east side of the house at the end of the porch where the hollyhocks are and where I try so hard to make morning glories grow. Even when I string twine from a stake in the ground to the porch roof for those darn morning glory vines, I only manage to get a few puny vines at best.

In the spring, the female pigeons lay a few little brown speckled eggs in the cozy spot where the two barn roofs meet. The eggs are about one-third the size of the eggs of our Rhode Island Red hens. I try not to go up there too often to check to see if the eggs are hatched because the mother pigeons seem to get upset when anybody is around them. I so want to see them hatch. It seems to take such a long time before the baby pigeons break out of their eggshell homes, but it is only soon after that they are trying to fly. A couple of times, they were trying so hard to fly that I tried to help them out. I was able to get close enough to the chicks, with their wobbly legs and their unsteady flutter of wings, so that I could give them a gentle toss in the air. Sometimes it helped them to fly and sometimes it didn't.

Near the pigeons' nests is an opening to outdoors that is about three feet square. This is the place the pigeons use to fly in and out of the barn. Under this opening is a good hiding place. There is a long, slanted area that is part of the roof over the part of the very old south barn where all the old cutter and rusted machinery are. Under the roof and over the first floor, the space is about three feet high, then it slants down to the first floor, which is ten feet away. It continues at those heights for about fifty feet into the darkness, but how long can any kid stay in there even if somebody is chasing her? Anybody hiding sooner or later has to come out, so there really isn't much use in hiding for very long. But it is one of my best hiding places in my dreams.

Actually, whenever I have some awful dreams of running and hiding from some terrible things like huge snakes, or going to be beat up or killed, my dreams always take me to that hiding place or another of my best hiding places—what everybody calls the mothball closet. It opens to the hall at the head of the front stairs of our house. It is an L-shaped closet about four feet long then five feet going right and about two and one-half feet wide. In the summertime it holds our winter clothes, which are put into mothballs. In winter, the mothball smell is okay as long as a kid doesn't go to school where the smell of mothballs is stronger than all the other smells—farm clothes; burning wood; black, oily floors; crayons; and whatever.

At the far end of the closet is a big wooden box. In the box are used clothes and a bag of about thirty tennis balls that my Aunt Clarinda got from the rich Buffalo people who go to the same Catholic Church she does. When we lose a ball, we can take another ball out—but only when my mother says we can. Sometimes on a Sunday, when nobody is supposed to work at anything that isn't very important (like milking cows or bringing in hay that has been cut and is going to be rained on, or it's a time to pray), we play ball in the yard in front of the house. That sure doesn't seem to happen very often. I wish we had books to read at home. All there is around the house is the *Sacred Heart Messenger* magazine and a Catholic newspaper.

In the beginning, when there weren't so many kids, we had a croquet set to play with. I can remember when we stuck the U-shaped metal hoops into the ground in different places on the front lawn. We used long-handled wooden mallets to smack a wooden ball about two times the size of a tennis ball through the course of hoops.

Sometimes, after the barn chores are finished, we manage to get to play with a baseball bat and a tennis ball. It seems as if every time we just get started, though, Ma comes to the door to call us in for prayers. By the time we're finished with the rosary, all the acts of contrition, novenas, and everything added on, there isn't one single speck of daylight left. I so love my turn at bat. If Ma calls us in for prayers just before my turn comes, and we have to go into the house right away, I feel awfully bad. Sometimes it's as if she thinks that having a good time is a sin. I am the best hitter and runner of the girls, so I guess I am the one who is probably the unhappiest to be called in for the prayers—especially since, during most of the time while saying prayers, we have to be on our knees.

The third hiding place that I use most often in my dreams is the attic, which is safer than the mothball closet. To get to it, you have to go through a two-foot-square opening in the hall ceiling just outside the mothball closet. The opening is covered by a square piece of wood that you have to push up and sideways, so it's much harder to get into than the closet. Being a kid, there is no way I can get into the attic without having something to stand on. In my dreams, when I somehow manage to get to the attic and pull the cover back over the opening, I often wake up still scared and breathing hard. My big brother Sam often chases me to hit me in my dreams, and, if he keeps looking for me, he will probably think of my very best place in the house to hide. Quite often in real life he chases me and hits me. There are a lot of times when he scares me.

One time Ma brought down from the attic some wonderful pattern books that belonged to Dad's sisters. Anybody going into the attic has to be very careful. There is no floor—just beams, and the second floor ceiling under the beams. I know how mad Ma and probably Dad would get if I ever sneaked up to the attic without permission, and then stepped off a beam and through the ceiling of the second floor! I'm sure a thin lower tree branch of the very big tree in the front yard would be used to punish me.

The pattern books are full of pictures of women in dresses that start under the chin then go down to puffed out big boobs. There is a little puff at the top of long, form-fitting sleeves that go all the way down the arm to the wrist. The waists are very small, and they look even smaller to us big-for-our-age farm kids. The skirts under the tiny middles are straight down from the waist in front, and, in back, the behind sticks out over the dress part, which drags on the ground. There are lacy designs over parts or most of the dresses.

I know from Ma's pictures of herself as a girl that she never wore dresses like that. Hers ended somewhere below the knee and above the ankle, but closer to the ankle, so these patterns are from a time before my mother was a girl. We have quite a few pictures of Ma and sometimes Dad with kids up to about the fifth one—me. After that, there seem to be fewer and fewer pictures of our family together. We keep our family pictures in the buffet in the dining room.

15

Lots of Kids ~ The Well

I wish Ma was more like our neighbor Mrs. Smith, who never raises her voice. But, of course, that could be because Mrs. Smith has only one kid. Actually, I don't really know how my mother could be like her with all us kids. There is never any talk in our family about what men and women do together, but we sure know that the only reason men and women get married is to have kids. I don't think Ma and Dad like each other very much. They never kiss or hug or say smoochy things to each other. I am always hoping that they will.

Having enough hot or even warm water for baths and for washing clothes is very hard with a lot of kids. Dad fixed it so that a very big water tank in the cellar of our house has a valve that, when opened, lets water into the tank. When the tank is full, we have to shut off the valve. The water for both the barn and the house comes from a well that is about one-eighth of a mile in back of the barn. The water from the well goes into a big, old, wooden, boxlike frame about six feet by eight feet and six feet down into the earth. Water gurgles up from its dirt floor. At the bottom of the north side of this box there is a strainer at the end of a rather large pipe. From the well, the pipe goes underground on the way to the big tank in the barn that stores the water for the house and supplies water for the animals.

The walls of the well are a sort of a slimy looking mix of wet mossy green sticking to boards and cement that sure doesn't look very strong. The top is covered with boards that have shrunken and dried to an ash gray color. They sag from each side to the middle and are full of knots and some skinny, long cracks. From the middle of summer to the fall, when I lean over the cement side and look down through the skinny cracks between the boards, I can see rather shallow, gently flowing water moving strands of stringy, very pale green, grasslike growth. I can also see slimy-looking, greenish brown, moss-covered, small rocks and murky-looking earth.

The well has a lingering smell that reminds me of the smell of the mysterious forest with its layers of dead leaves. When there has been plenty of rain and snow, there isn't any reason to worry, but when there hasn't been much rain and snow, things can get pretty bad. Sometimes the water level in the well gets very close to the bottom. The drinking water for the house becomes a little cloudy, and, once in a while, a little live wiggly something finds its way to our chipped ceramic drinking cups. That's when everybody worries.

To get water to the barn and house, first we pump water from the well with a big electric pump in the barn to the big water tank in the barn. The tank is about two feet off the cement floor in front of the cows on the north side of the barn, and just before the door to the milk house. To get water to the house, first we have to open the water tank valve in the cellar of the house, then we have to open the valve to the pipe that goes from the tank in the barn to the tank in the house. Then we have to turn on the pump motor. When the house tank is full, some-body has to go back to the barn to close the valve and turn off the pump, then back to the house to close the valve on the tank in the cellar.

Boy, with all that back and forth, there are many times when we miss a step and there is no running water in the house for a little while. When the cellar tank is finally filled, we fill the upright, round, six-foot-high water tank next to the wood-burning stove in the kitchen. The water is then warmed by the stove, which takes quite a while. That is the tank that supplies warm water to the two bathrooms and to the kitchen and washroom sinks. We never know whether the water in the kitchen stove water reservoir, which holds a few gallons, or the water in the kettle will be cold or empty.

Quite often, when some kid or Ma wants warm water for washing dishes, washing clothes, or taking a bath there will be no warm water. That can be because somebody used all the warm water for a bath, or because the water hasn't been pumped to the house from the barn. I often do all the turning on and off without being told. It seems to me that the other kids never do the water turning on and off without Ma having to keep after them to get it started. Then she yells all the way to the last part of the job—turning off the pump. Of course, my brothers and sisters might not think what I say is true.

The poor pump. So many times when I go to the barn, there it is groaning and straining away as it tries to pump more water into the houses full tank. The motor pumps all the water for the animals and our big family. With all that push-ing, I don't know how it keeps going year after year. It seems to be working so very hard when the tanks are already full. Of course, I go running to turn it off when I hear the pitiful sound. I guess maybe the other kids do too.

Even though I like working in the barn much better than the house, I sure help in the house with one job without being told—and that is washing clothes.

There are enough things for kids at school to be mean to us about without giving them one more—my family wearing dirty clothes. Actually, it seems to me I do a lot of things in the barn and quite a few in the house without being told. The washing machine is in the washroom, which is in the southeast corner of the house. It has legs about twelve inches long that support a large tub. There are rollers for wringing out the wet clothes on an arm that has three settings and can be moved around. The first setting of the roller arm is between the washing machine and the first rinse tub. The wash water goes back into the washing machine as we put the clothes through the wringer into the first rinse tub. Next, we position the roller arm between the two rinse tubs, and we move clothes around in the first rinse tub. We put the clothes through the rollers into the second rinse tub. Next, we position the roller arm between the second rinse tub and an oval wicker clothes basket that sits on the floor. We swish the clothes around in the second rinse tub, then we put them through the roller to the basket.

One of the doors in the washroom leads out to the east end of the porch. The playhouse is about twenty feet off the end of the porch, and a clothesline runs south from the playhouse and along the driveway: two T-shaped poles hold four twenty-foot cotton rope clotheslines between them. South of the clothesline, extending for another twenty feet along the driveway, is a thick bunch of rose bushes that produce small pink roses that have a wonderful, dainty, heavenly smell surrounding them.

Past the pink rosebushes is a small maple tree in the middle of a twenty-five-foot row of currant bushes. Ma uses the currants for making a delicious pink jelly. When the jelly is cooked just long enough, she pours it into little glass jars while its still very hot and then seals the jars with a one-third-inch layer of melted paraffin. It sure doesn't take long before goodies like that are all gone. Beyond the currant bushes, there are the wild horseradish plants that have coarse green tops and white, carrotlike roots. My eyes water when we grind up the white roots, and all over inside my head burns when I eat it. Our oldest brother Sam, Junior, is the only person who doesn't seem to mind his eyes watering or how eating horseradish makes him feel. We kids sure don't eat much horseradish. Eating it is another example of the things that Sam, Junior, does that most kids—and even some grown-ups—don't want to do.

There is a cherry tree next to the woodshed in back of the house. When the cherries get ripe, it's a race between the birds and the kids for the cherries. The birds seem to be the winners most of the time. They can check from the air every single day to see if the berries are ready. There are some wild cherry trees that grow at the base of a stone wall all the way in the back of the house on the northern border of our farm. The Dominick farm fields begin on the other side. West and across the dirt road from the field is our schoolhouse. On the south side of the schoolhouse is some Trombley family land, and on the west and north sides of the schoolhouse and the playground is more Dominic farmland.

Practically as soon as any kid is able to talk, Ma and Dad make sure they take "the pledge." Well, maybe not quite that soon. Part of the pledge is that we will never have evil drinks like beer or stronger stuff. Drinking provides a perfect opportunity for the devil to help us do bad things. Sam, Junior, in one way or another, sometimes manages to get around that. Sam picks the wild cherries next to the stone wall and somehow he gets the juice out of the cherries into one-quart bottles and fastens down the top with cork stoppers that have metal clamps. I don't know what he puts in with the cherries and sugar and water. A few months later, when he loosens the cap of one of the bottles in the kitchen sink, there is stuff that flies all over. I'm not sure there is anything in those bottles but spoiled wild cherry juice. It sure is exciting to watch Sam open a bottle, knowing the noise and mess that is sure to follow. Once I tried a taste. It was awful.

I don't know why my mother and father don't say anything to Sam about so many things he does, like going to a bar to drink beer. I sometimes hear my mother and father whispering about some of what must be pretty awful things that happen in bars. No matter how mean he is to me, like hitting me, or if he doesn't kneel up straight or kneel at all during prayers, they don't say anything. I guess most of us kids, in our hearts, know why. He is the first, the oldest, and the only boy followed by us five girls. That by itself is enough in a farm family, which so needs boys for very heavy chores that girls can't do, to treat the boys like favorites. Oh well, I do my best. Except for the fact that I can't do the heavy chores, my dad probably would have liked me even more than the boys. I'm not sure he doesn't anyway.

A few feet east of the cherry bushes next to the house and northeast of the playhouse is a place on the edge of the hayfield where trash that is going to be burned is thrown on the ground. There isn't much to throw out. Farm people can things like tomatoes in reusable glass jars with glass covers, so the only thing we throw out is the rubber sealing ring that is placed on the glass lip at the top of the jar before the glass top is put on. Practically the only paper we have comes from a couple of monthly or weekly Catholic magazines like the one that a priest writes letting us know all about the evil in communist doctrine—and another one is the *Sacred Heart Messenger*. I sure wish we would get the kind of magazines the Smith's get, like the *Saturday Evening Post* and *Life*. But, if we got those, we might get some ideas that might be sinful, and we might very well become not very good Catholics.

I don't know if Dad had a say in this, but, for a while, all the way back when I was a very little kid, Ma made me stand on the steps of St. Edmund's Church in Ellenburg Corners selling a Catholic paper or magazine. There I was, hoping and praying real hard that a few people would see my awfully unhappy face and buy one of the copies I was holding. Please, God, and then I could leave those steps and not be one of the Patnode kids doing something that no city kid ever does or, for that matter, any other kid from other families ever does. But Ma and Dad are determined. It sure isn't going to be their fault if we don't make it to heaven. After all, spreading the faith is part of any good Catholic's job, no matter how young.

Boy, Ma and Dad are going to be able to add up all the things they make us do—the masses, the confessions, the pledges of faith, offering up all our good thoughts and deeds, all the rosaries, stations of the cross, the catechism. I wonder if there is such a thing as a certain wonderful place in heaven for someone who has so many good things to add up. Would they more than make up for any bad things that we kids or they might do?

I know that our four aunts, who are Benedictine nuns in St. Marys, Pennsylvania, all think people are on this earth to suffer, because they believe that God in his goodness is going to reward them with eternal happiness in the next world. I don't know the exact words, but we sure are told enough times that the more you suffer on earth, the more you will be rewarded in the next world. Some ideas like that are hard to figure out. Isn't it okay to just want to try and be happy and want to be liked? Somehow, the need to suffer never seems right to me. In my heart of hearts, with all the hitting and hollering, I just know that I can be liked and maybe be happy with other people someplace else.

A couple of people told me in secret that Sam and I are the only ones that are "okay" in the Sam Patnode family. It is pretty awful to hear that about my family, but I know better than to tell anybody. What a ruckus that would cause. Maybe it's because I never go back to my mother and father and tell them anything that is said or done if I know it will make them mad. I think Sam does the same thing. I don't tell them about how girls have to take off their top clothes and only have a little triangle diaperlike cloth to try and cover their boobs for school exams. And I don't tell them that we are taught that the earth is made in some way other than by God, or that, in the big school, girls take showers together. Boy, things like that make my parents real mad, and I just know that a teacher or the superintendent they call Dictator Pumpkin, or somebody else, would get an earful.

One time, Ross and Clarence came to school with some very exciting news—a two-headed calf had been born on their farm. It was still alive when we heard about it. I so much wanted to go and see it, but we weren't allowed. I expect my parents see the work of the devil even in a two-headed calf. The calf died before I could find a way to see it. Well, maybe there never would have been a way. If I went to the farm, I would have had to go past a couple of other farmhouses where I might have been seen, and Ma might have heard about it. Probably Clarence's father would not have let me go into his barn anyway, because most people know how my mother and father are.

One of the things that make my parents different from other parents is that they complain to the teacher about every little thing; for example, if it takes us too long to get home from school, they always suspect we may have gotten into some kind of bad mischief. Then, on top of that, they don't let us play at our neighbors' houses—not even my brothers, who are allowed to get away with a lot more things than we girls.

Actually, kids aren't welcome at our house, either. If they could come to our house, it would be expected that we could go to their houses. If we went to their houses, who knows what bad things might be going on. And, even if there weren't any bad things going on, Mom and Dad have to think about the future no matter whose house we are at. Just think, if we became friends with a kid who is a bad Catholic—one who doesn't go to Sunday mass and confession—or maybe who isn't even a Catholic, we might stay friends for a long time. We might even fall in love and want to marry that friend! We could all end up going to hell.

16

Neighbors ~ Runaway Horses

Most of us kids go barefoot in the summertime. Of course, we always have shoes for church and school. Some of the other farm families are worse off than we Sam and Jeannette Patnode kids. There are some farm kids, especially the ones who live farther up the dirt road from us, who sometimes don't wear underwear, even in winter. Other kids can tell because sometimes there is a hole in their overalls, usually in the knees or bottoms. They come from a family that has a couple of sons in World War II. We see stars on the American flags that people hang in the windows of their houses. Each star means they have a kid in the war. We heard that a family gets ten thousand dollars if a soldier son dies in the war. One kid who hadn't been wearing underwear started to wear new boots and clothes. I felt bad, but it sure isn't anything anybody talks about. Nobody ever said anything—not Miss Carpenter, and certainly not any of us.

Another farmer family—the one that lives about a quarter mile west of our house and down their own dirt road—had another one of those awful things happen. They are a Shalo family. Some of the kids have only fuzz for hair and thick, protruding nails. One of their daughters was about twelve years old. She was mowing a hayfield with a team of horses. A hay mower has a big, five-foot cutter blade with little triangles that slice back and forth at ground level. Her little brother came running over to her. I don't know how it happened, but somehow one of his legs got cut off below the knee. That's about all we kids ever heard about that awful accident.

When a farmer friend learned that it's my job to rake hay with the help of a horse, he told me another farm story. It is about a woman who is an aunt to the Lashway kids. Her horse ran away when she was raking hay. She had been using the same kind of rake that I use. It has two big, three-foot-high spoked wheels on each side, with a seat that sits over C-shaped teeth between the wheels. When this woman was a kid, the horse ran away with her on the rake with its teeth in the down position. She fell to the ground in back of the horse and into the teeth of the rake. The horse galloped into a stone wall with barbed wire fencing. The stones jerked the teeth enough so it dropped her at the stone wall. The story went on that she was badly hurt, but she looked okay to us kids.

One time, my father, my brother Sam, our hired man Howard, and I took a team of horses up the LaClair road to get some hay from our hayfield that is on the southernmost portion of our land. Nobody but the LaClairs live at the end of the one-and-one-half-mile-long dirt road with its many large, mostly flat rocks and deep ruts. Cars almost never go down that road because it's so easy to get stuck in the mud or snow, or for rocks to gouge the underside of a car. The road is not plowed all winter long, so the LaClair kids are snowed in a lot longer than we are, and we are snowed in for about a month and a half.

We first went the quarter mile east down our dirt road, then right going south down the LaClair road. On that corner is a small, ramshackle, one-and-one-half-story house with broken windows where nobody lives. We were told to never go inside because floors or staircases might collapse. Somehow, empty houses make our mother and father very uneasy. I think that sin is somehow mixed up in their thinking. One time, Rose and I managed to go inside and look around. If she was with me doing something that we were not supposed to be doing, I knew she wouldn't tell on me.

Down the road to our most southerly hayfield, we went past our good hayfield on the right. The Miller farm pasture is on the left. Farther down the road on the right is our night pasture with all the rocks and low-lying brush and some small blueberry bushes a few inches high. The odd thing in the night pasture, which is almost just rocks and no trees, a place ringed by stone walls topped by a barbed wire fence with a few raspberry bushes, is a pile of bones. They probably are cow's bones. We never asked what they were doing there. On farms, kids don't ask many questions no matter how curious they are.

After the night pasture is one of our hayfields with its scrawny growth of hay, among which are plants that are really just weeds like flowering colorful paint-brushes and buttercups. This field is far away from the barn, so it's no wonder that it isn't like the ones closer to the barn and house. It is never plowed, fertil-ized, or planted with crops like oats. There already is too much work to do in the fields around the house and barn. The southernmost field is where, sometime in late spring, I am able to get a whole cup of wild strawberries. That doesn't hap-pen very often because the tiny berries are the sweetest and the most delicious in the world to eat straight from the tiny strawberry plants, so the biggest share never makes it to a cup. When I finally do get one cup of berries, I try to get enough eggs to make a white cake. Then we make frosting with the strawberries, one egg white, and one cup of sugar. It sure is a wonderful treat.

Across the distant hayfield is the small stream that runs north through our night pasture, then through our day pasture, and on through the Smith's day pasture, and then their night pasture. I don't know where it goes from there. When we got to the hay fields, Dad told me to hold the reins of the team of horses that was fastened to the hay wagon while the men went to turn over some hay in the field across the little stream. I was pretty little and I sort of fiddled around with the reins. The team took off at a very fast gallop. Boy, was I scared.

I was so busy hanging on to the wagon that I dropped the reins. I already knew that when horses run away they are kind of crazy, and I sure wasn't strong enough to pull the reins hard enough to make them stop. Runaway horses will gallop full speed into stone fences, barbed wire, or whatever is in front of them. Our horses sure bounced me around as they galloped straight through the rocky bottom of the stream and on into the second half of the hayfield. My father screamed for Howard, who managed to run fast enough to get the horses stopped by the far end of the field. After that, I guess my father knew I was too little to handle a team of horses because it sure didn't get to be another of my regular jobs on the farm.

Last year, I had my first driving lesson on a motorized vehicle—a Cletrac tractor, which is our first tractor. It sure looked awfully big. The tractor has tracks instead of regular wheels. My brother Sam made me climb aboard. He attached a harrow and told me I was to harrow in the field in back of the house. This implement digs into the ground with curved hooks and loosens the soil before planting. He pointed to the two handles in front of the seat. The handles are at the end of metal bars that go all the way into the floorboards. I was to push both handles forward to make the tractor go forward and pull both back to back up. I was to pull on the right handle to go right and the left handle to go left. The brake is a foot pedal.

With a few jerks here and there, I learned to drive the tractor, but the bad part of harrowing or plowing is the darn rocks and the woodchuck holes. Rocks that are embedded in the ground catch on the earth-turning, foot-high hooks of the harrow. And woodchuck holes are bad to get stuck in—because of the chance of breaking something on the harrow.

In the spring, after the earth has been freshly turned over by a harrow or a plow before anything is planted, comes that job I told you about when all the kids have to run after the stoneboat and fill it with all the newly-exposed rocks as it is dragged through the fields by a horse. As I mentioned, this is one of the worst jobs on the farm, and most kids try to find something else to do when they are told to help. I don't know how this happens, but the winter freezing and the summer thaw push up quite a few stones to the top of the dirt. There seem to be so many things that happen on a farm to make extra work. I wonder ... when I grow up, will I ever want to live on a farm?

17

Ma and Dad ~ Lent

I wonder if other kids think very much about heaven or hell or whether they are good or bad. I really do try to be a good girl, but then Rose is such a Goody Two-shoes, and I don't want to be like her. With her, whatever Ma says, it's always okay. I'm sure she doesn't take showers with other kids or try to flirt with boys. She and I are the same age for one week. She is older than I am by fifty-one weeks. It's a good thing she seems to like me so much, or I sure would be very jealous of her and probably would almost hate her. She has perfect teeth, long black hair, and a pretty face. She is Ma's pet. Oh well—I think that I'm Dad's pet. I guess that pretty much makes up for her being Ma's pet.

In the spring there sure is some excitement. As soon as the snow melts, and the trees and the grass turn green, a gang of people come down the road from the east past our house then turn north. Ma says they are gypsies. They form a parade—a couple of covered wagons, grown-ups and kids, big horses, and darling little Shetland ponies. The wagons look as if they are chock-full, and there are things hanging from them that swing as the wagons bounce along. The people wear loose-fitting, colorful clothes. I can't figure out where they come from or where they are going. Nobody in my family, or any of the other families around us, knows either. Sometimes, at the end of summer when it starts getting cold, I see them going back in the other direction.

Lots of times we kids stay at Ma's mother's house. She is our grandma Augusta Langevin. She sure is strict. Out of her eleven kids, four of her girls—my aunts—are nuns. She so much wanted one of her four boys to be a priest, especially since priests are the ones who take the place of God on earth. That sure would help her to get an even higher place in heaven—if that can happen.

Grandma sure doesn't have to tell us how proud she is of her four nun daughters. Their pictures are everywhere in every house she ever lives in. The four nun aunts wear black laced shoes with thick, one-and-one-half-inch rubber heels, long black dresses with a large white starched bib, and a black veil over their white-covered forehead. Only their eyes, cheeks, nose, mouth, chin, and hands are visible. I wonder what they wear underneath.

I heard my father say that, when his parents, Grandmother and Grandfather Patnode, were living, they spelled their last name "Patenaude." Both of them died before I was born, so I never got to know them. My father is eighteen years older than my mother. We all know about Dad having gone with Katie White for eighteen years before he married my mother. Miss White is a school teacher who lives with her mother in Ellenburg Depot. I think the fact that she lives with her mother had something to do with why she didn't marry my father. Both Katie White and my mother are Catholic Daughters of America. I wonder what they say to each other when they meet.

Quite often, when my mother and father are mad at each other, my mother will say something about other women having told her that, if they had known that my father had stopped dating Katie White, they would have put their hat in the ring for him. Then Ma adds that, if she had known that one of them was interested, they sure could have had him! I expect that having had so many kids, as well as having to keep all of us fed, then trying to keep worldly temptations away from us in order to try to make sure we all go to heaven, is pretty hard work. Even though I think about things like that, it makes me feel really bad to have her say mean things about my father.

What a big job both my mother and father have. I think that probably the hardest thing in life for them is what they call "being a good Catholic." Even I know that the only time that people are supposed to get very close together is to make babies. I'm not sure how I know that—I just do. I can imagine what it must be like for farmers' wives, especially since a lot of farmers don't take a bath every day, even with all the chores they do from very early morning to late in the evening.

Between having so many kids, Dad having so many barn chores, and Ma taking care of new babies as well as some bigger ones, trying to make sure that clothes and other things are washed as well as the dishes, it's no wonder that Ma and Dad don't seem to like each other very much.

I don't know much about mothers and fathers and how babies are made, but I sure do know how much bigger our family is compared to all the other kids' families. Sometimes I hear a kind of whispered, making-fun kind of laugh coming from other kids about my family. Of course, something like that could mean more than one thing—such as the size of my family or the way my mother hollered at somebody in the school system about something like the lies they teach in school. I so much want my family to be more like other families.

For a while, after a baby is born in my house, my mother sleeps on a bed with a feather mattress on it that is set up in front of the fireplace in the parlor. There is a big four-foot-square window in the parlor that overlooks the porch. There is a six-inch border of beautiful colored glass running along the top of the window, and there are crisp, lacy, starched curtains over it. There is another regular-size window next to the fireplace with the same kind of curtains. At the foot of the bed is the baby's crib. During that time, my father sleeps in their second-floor bedroom that is at the head of the back stairs. The bedroom has a stovepipe running through it from the first floor bathroom, where there is a little four-legged woodstove that sits on a table in the corner between the bathtub and toilet. The little stove helps to keep the bedroom the warmest bedroom in the house.

The same second-floor bedroom has a window that I look out of when I'm waiting for the school bus to come down the road toward our house.

My mother and father's second-floor bedroom has a rather large closet with a slanted ceiling that goes from the height of the bedroom ceiling down to three feet. There is a trunk in the middle of the far wall, shelves on the right side, and hooks for clothes on the other walls of the closet. The closet is the place I try to get to before any other kid gets to claim it on Good Friday. We kids are expected to find a dark place for three hours of meditation. The three hours represent the three hours of Christ's suffering on the cross. If we are going to go to heaven when we die, there are certain things we need to do. Every once in a while, another kid beats me to the closet. One time, my meditation place was the shoe and boot closet of the washroom on the first floor. The three hours seemed as if they would never end. The next year I made sure I was the first kid in the bedroom closet.

In order to get extra blessings, I always take a rosary with me and spend at least part of the time praying as well as meditating on how good God is—things like that. A good way to be able to pray and meditate and know all the wonder of Christ's suffering for us is to make the stations of the cross at our St. Edmund's Church in Ellenburg Corners. Every kid needs to do penance during Lent to better understand God's suffering and be happy about the idea of his resurrection at Easter time.

The three hours alone in a dark place seem so very long, but one good thing is that Ma always has steaming hot, homemade vegetable soup with crackers ready for us at the end. On top of that, at last it is the end of the forty days of Lent, so we don't have to keep doing or not doing whatever we had promised for Lent. During Lent, I work extra hard at having no sins in thought and deed for all of the forty days, as well as try to do good things like being very nice to people I don't like. At last, Easter Sunday comes. No matter how poor we are, there is a hidden Easter basket for the littlest kids to find and from which the bigger kids try and get some candy. After it's all over, even all the kneeling during Lent doesn't seem so bad.

18

Chickens and Skunks

Boy, when winter comes, it sure is good to have the glass quart jars of tomatoes and other things that Ma puts up in the fall. We kids help her with the canning, except when she uses the steamer, which is a large, box-shaped tin about eighteen inches square and two and one-half feet high. In the front there are two little doors, one over the other. Behind each door is a wire shelf. Under the bottom shelf is space for a couple inches of water. Ma puts the steamer on top of the stove with water in the bottom. She then loads about nine quart jars on each little shelf. After the water starts to boil and the steamer is full of steam, the jars have to stay inside for a certain length of time to make sure they don't spoil during the long, cold winter ahead. Ma uses the steamer not only for canning, but also for cooking stuffed chickens.

Even though we have chickens on our farm, we don't get to eat chicken very often, because we need them for eggs. Chickens are kind of funny. They start out so cute. Ma orders them from some place far away. They come in a big flat box about two feet by two feet and five inches deep with small holes in the cover. She always gets Rhode Island Reds, which lay big brown eggs, unlike white hens, which lay much smaller white eggs. There are always a couple of dead chicks by the time we open the box. It is so exciting—except for the couple of dead chicks already stepped on and wet and smelly. There are usually about seventy-five little balls of yellow fluff chirping away. I don't know why the chicks are yellow when they are little and then, by the time they are big hens, they have grown a feather coat of shiny rust red.

By the time the chicks get to us, it's as if they can't wait to get out of their little prison. The bottom of the box is covered with soaking wet strips of paper and their little squishy poops. After all, they have to potty on the way to our house. The first thing we have to do is to get them from the cardboard box and into their own little wood-framed house. A forty-watt bulb with a cover of wire mesh is put inside their new home. The mesh keeps the little chicks from pushing each

112

other against the bulb as they try to get next to its warmth. Every one of them tries to get near the bulb. It's no wonder, after their long trip with no heat and no light except maybe through the little holes in the box. I don't like to think about their trip.

How can the cutest little babies change so quickly? By the time all the chicks' yellow fluff is gone and the feathers are starting to come in, they sure look different and are not very pretty—they are gangly and scrawny looking with short feathers. You can see a little bit of skin between their feathers, and all of them try to be so grown up. Already, there are certain ones I can tell are going to be the bosses. They are the first ones to get to the corn or grain we toss to the ground from a bucket. During the summer, the growing chicks, as well as the full-grown hens, run around the grounds between the barn and the one-car garage and next to the road.

The hens' winter house is in the very big, east end of the barn, which looks like a house and is attached to the middle part. We kids know about north and south and east and west. Grown-ups often talk in winter about the bitterly cold north wind, which, of course, comes from the north. We also learn about geography and directions in school.

As I have said, the east and west ends of the barn are much older than the middle part where the cows are. Parts of the east end were used for other animals a long time before we used it for chickens and pigs. As you go into that part of the barn, first there is a very big space, which is the entire first floor, with great big doors that go to the outside. On top of it is a one-and-one-half-story loft under a pitched roof, where the straw is blown in when we separate the oat from the straw. Then there is another big double door that goes into the newer middle part, where the cows, horses, calves, and sometimes even a chained dog are.

The big space in the east barn first floor has nothing in the middle because that is where the horses are harnessed together to be driven outside and hitched up to farm wagons or whatever. There is a very old car with open sides in one corner, which looks a lot like a very old buggy. That car has never been used as far back as any of us kids can remember. It has broken, lanternlike headlights and a dried-up and cracked gray leather seat—and, of course, cobwebs. There aren't nearly as many cobwebs around this part of the barn as there are farther back where not very many kids and no grown-ups explore. Under the seat of the old car is a wonderful place for hens to hide while they lay their eggs.

In other parts of the big space there are a tractor, a cutter, and other things that need to be fixed, but probably never will be. Some of that machinery has been there for a very long time. The area is kind of messy. There are some things that my dad just can't get to do. There are always special things that have to be done pretty fast, like mending a broken harness or making new shoes for a horse. Then, of course, there are all the chores that can't wait, like milking the cows, feeding all the animals, cleaning out the manure, bringing in the hay and oats in summer—all those things always have to come first. There just are so many things to do.

An opening in the big room that probably had a door at one time leads to where the chickens are kept. After you go through this opening, on the left is a small, eight-foot-square space with walls. It is one of the places I use in my dreams when I am trying to get away from a bad person or a snake because it has a ladder on one wall to get to the second floor. In fact, if I go up that ladder, I can get to every part of the barn—up and down the two old end parts and the newer middle part.

After the space with the ladder is another small, roomlike place that is enclosed except for one side that is made of very old chicken wire. It sure has never been used for our chickens. It is just another space that was probably used for something like chickens or calves or pigs a very long time ago. Next to the wire fencing is the door to where the chickens are. I can tell that the space was used for three horses. There are three spaces that are the same shape and size as Ned and Kit's stalls in the newer part of the barn.

At the far end of the horse stalls is what looks like moldy old wooden mangers that have been nailed to the wall. The bases are attached to the wall about a foot from the floor and the sides slant out as they rise three feet from the floor to the open tops. The mangers look like the feeding troughs in front of some of the animals in pictures of the barn where Mary had little baby Jesus. The mangers hold musty decaying heaps of what was probably hay or straw. I guess the horses' water must have been brought in by buckets because there are no water pipes in the stalls.

In the winter, it sure gets awfully cold in the chicken house. There are no other animals in that part of the barn to help keep it a little warmer. Sometimes I feel really bad about the poor grownup Rhode Island Reds. During the winter, they have only one bucket of water to drink from. The top of the water freezes overnight, so every day they have to get fresh water. When it's bitter cold, with a raging wind getting through all the little spaces into the henhouse, and we think we'll probably have some potatoes left over when spring comes, Dad cooks up a big bucket of steaming potatoes for those poor cold hens.

By winter, they are full grown and wearing their covering of reddish brown feathers with a fluffier, featherlike down underneath the long outer feathers.

When we kill the chickens to eat, we often save the inner fluffy feathers to stuff inside homemade pillows made of ticking. The rooster has a big, red comb on top of his head and long tail feathers. They all have long, coarse, reddish brown feathers on their wings, and the hens' feathers are a little shorter on their tails. I don't know how this happens, but one or two of the little yellow fluffy chicks always turn into big roosters instead of hens. When the roosters are cooped up with the hens in winter, things sure can get ugly. All any kid does in the henhouse is look all over trying to find where the hens lay their eggs, but it's a good idea to look first to see where the rooster might be.

One of the special places that we know to check for eggs is in the manger at the head of the horse stalls, while, at the same time, keeping a lookout for that big ugly red rooster. Once my sister Gemma didn't look well enough for the rooster. There she was, all the way in the stall with the rooster all mad and fluffed up jumping up and down making all kinds of mean rooster noises. My sister was screaming really loud. Of course, my father came running with a pitchfork to get the rooster away from her. There are three box-shaped nests about eighteen inches square and two feet deep, and open in front that were built many years ago for the hens as a special place to lay their eggs. The boxes are nailed to the wall three feet up from the floor, and have some straw in the bottom.

But hens are funny. If they have a chance, they like to hide their eggs, and sometimes they even get away with it. Once, a hen managed to not only lay a few eggs, but hatch them at the bottom of what had been an old well in another part of the old barn. It is past where the chickens are, and even past where our pigs once were. Now there aren't any animals—just darkness, hanging gray cobwebs, thick dust, musty smells, a falling-down floor, and broken windows. One day I was in the chicken house and heard wonderful little chicks' chirpy noises far away. It took a while to find the chicks. The only light was from where windows had been or spaces in the walls to outside, so it was hard to see.

When I finally found the area where the soft little chirps were coming from, I still couldn't see them. As it was, I could barely see the three-foot hole in the floor, but I was pretty sure that's where they were—at the bottom of the hole. My father told me that the hole was where there had been a well a very long time ago. It took a lot of crying and coaxing to get my father away from his regular chores and get him to get a ladder to go into the well and get the darling little chicks and their mother out of there. I can't figure out how she managed to lay the eggs and then sit on them till they hatched all the way down at the bottom of the old well.

Another time a hen managed to hide her eggs so well that there was a family of nine little yellow chicks just out of their shells at the wrong time of year! It was fall, and they would die if we put them in the very cold part of the barn where the big hens were. This was another one of those times that things turned out wonderfully—only this time it was Ma I had to coax. Even now, I can't believe she let me keep them in the washroom of the house. I got a very thin, wooden-walled bushel basket—the kind the tomatoes for canning come in. I got an extension cord and put a ten-watt bulb on the end, then put it through a cardboard and cloth cover I made up, then into the bushel basket to keep the chicks warm. I had to make sure to keep them fed and watered, and I had to change the bedding at the bottom of the basket quite often. It sure got crowded by the time they got a little bigger. I was so happy when at last I could let them out with the others.

Another time, there was a half-grown chicken that broke its leg above the scaly yellow in the meat and feather part. My father said I couldn't keep it alive with a break like that. My brother and sisters looked at me kind of funny when I asked one of them to hold the chick while I was working on its leg, but I did it anyway. I cut strips from an old white diaper and used little sticks to hold everything in place. It was so wonderful for me when the chick got better. After a while, I couldn't tell that one from the others.

There was a time when we had a lot of trouble with skunks. It was after my father built a summer henhouse for the chickens between the barn and the garage. It is made of wood with a slanted roof starting on a two-foot wall going to a height of about three feet on the other side, which faces south. The little building is about twenty feet long and four feet wide. The south side is where the opening is for the chickens to come and go.

There was some kind of animal stealing the chickens, only one or two at first, so by the time my father noticed he had to do something pretty fast. He started getting up earlier than usual to try and kill whatever was killing our chickens. He took his rifle or shotgun with him—the one from the high shelf in the washroom. At first nothing was happening, but finally he sure took care of what turned out to be skunks.

It was later in the morning when I found out about the four skunks my father had killed. It didn't take long to find out once I came downstairs, because the washroom was already full of the skunk smell, and the kitchen and bathroom next to the washroom were already starting to smell bad. Over and over, we washed and rinsed, washed and rinsed Dad's clothes. Skunks are mostly black with some white. They sure are pretty, but I couldn't think about that when the awful smell was so bad. I don't know how close he got to them to be able to shoot them, but they sure squirted him real good before they died. We kids heard that the only way to really get rid of the smell on skunk sprayed clothes is to bury them. Ma just kept washing the clothes over and over because we sure can't afford to just bury clothes because they smell.

I sure was proud of my father. I guess my dad was kind of proud too, because in the daylight, we saw all four of the skunks on top of the little wooden chicken house—stretched out and dead.

19

Killing and Dressing Chickens to Eat

Well, here I am again, talking about chickens. I'm getting to the part about chickens that is hard to talk about—killing and dressing them before eating them. Of course, the eating is wonderful because we don't kill chickens very often and they taste so good. In winter, when it gets very cold, hens don't lay very many eggs. Even in the summer, when they lay more eggs, there aren't enough so we can have family meals with eggs taking the place of meat. It seems as if the men get most of the eggs that the hens lay. Sometimes I manage to get a couple of eggs to make a cake.

I am so proud of my baking because I am the person who is the dessert maker in my family. One time, my whole family went to church except for the very littlest kid and me. I was a big girl of nine or ten, and I could bake and, at the same, time take care of the littlest kid. I used my usual recipe to make the pie crust. First, using a special utensil, I cut one cup of lard into three cups of flour and a pinch of salt and then kneaded it together with a little cold water. Next I pulled out the waist-high, three-by-two-foot, metal-over-wood sliding shelf that is part of our cupboard. I sprinkled the board with flour and rolled out dough.

I made a couple of single-crust pies, and there was some dough left over. I was very happy because I was able to make a lot of tarts, which are so very delicious when covered with jelly or jam. I very carefully rolled out the leftover dough then cut round little pieces the size of cookies. Next I made a little one third inch dough edge around each of the tarts.

I was able to make so many that a big metal tray—the one we use for baking cookies—was covered with them. It was to be a surprise for my mother, father, and all my brothers and sisters when they got back from church. They would put the homemade currant jelly on my little tarts and they would praise me. Well, almost for sure, not praise, but I was sure the tarts would all go in a hurry, which would be kind of like praise. I guess God punished me for my pride. In my excitement, I forgot them and, by the time I got them out of the oven, they were all burned so badly they even smoked a little.

Back to the chickens. If we are having chicken for a day like Christmas or Easter, we have to cook two chickens for our big family. Quite often, the only way we can have chicken is if one of us kids promises to do all the preparation to get them ready for cooking. It seems to me that I am often that kid, but I expect that some of my sisters, and even my mother would say the same thing. At any rate, my father and mother finally agree to a chicken dinner.

My father has to try and find a couple of hens that aren't laying eggs. He does that by feeling between their legs. He sure is awfully disappointed when he hasn't figured it right. When a hen is cut open, I can tell if it had been a laying hen because inside will be a few yolks that would have become eggs. There might be yolks the size of the ones inside regular eggs, and there might be some smaller than a marble. I don't know why there never is any egg white or shells inside the hens and around the yolk.

First, my dad leans his ax against a block of wood that sits between the barn and the garage that he uses for killing chickens. The block of wood is about two feet high and eighteen inches across and still has the bark around the outside. Then he picks out a hen and carries her out of the barn by her legs with the wings flapping all over the place. What a loud squawking racket the hen makes. I wonder if they know they are going to die. Dad carries the hen with two hands until he gets to the block of wood, and then he switches the hen's legs to one hand and reaches for the ax with the other. I have to turn away.

The sound gets more awful and then, all of a sudden, it's quiet. I turn back. Hens die in an awful way, with no head, jumping around spurting blood all over the white snow. The head lies on the ground next to the block of wood. I'm sure it doesn't take very long for the hen to stop jumping around with no head, but it seems to take such an awful long time. Is she feeling any pain? I guess she can't without a head. Finally, the hen falls to the ground with the last little flapping of her wings. Then Dad has to do it all over again with the second hen. I wish there was another way.

The next step is carrying the two hens to the washroom of the house for dressing. As you come into the washroom, on the left is a black metal sink that is about eighteen inches by three feet, and four inches deep. The lip of the metal sink rests on the edge of a rather narrow wooden board that stretches to small counterlike sideboards on both sides of the sink. The sink has hot and cold running water, and we leave an enamel washbasin in it to use for washing our hands after farm and garden chores. We also use the sink for scrubbing the dirt off vegetables like potatoes, beets, and carrots with a vegetable brush kept on the back of the sink.

The washroom sink is where the dead chickens land when they are brought into the house. We cover the shelves on both sides of the sink with some kind of paper cover. We boil water and pour it into a bucket in the sink. Holding the hens by their legs, we lower them into the very hot water for a few minutes to loosen their feathers. Then we remove the chickens to the sink to let the water drain from the feathers. The smell is pretty bad. Sometimes, if we are saving some of the softer feathers underneath the regular feathers for pillows, we pull out those feathers before the hens are put in the boiling water to loosen the coarser outer feathers. We use the shelf on the left for pulling out the feathers, then use the shelf on the other side of the sink for taking the insides out and cutting off the legs where the yellow scaly part meets the skin part.

In the front of a chicken is a little pouch where the grain and other food they eat first stops. I have to cut it out. Then I cut open the back of the hen, starting from the end of the ribs down to where the tail feathers were. Next I put my hand into the hen and pull out all the stuff inside. I'll bet city kids wouldn't do that even if they had to before they could eat the delicious chicken. It's not a very nice job, but it isn't so bad if I keep thinking about how good it is going to smell while it's cooking and how good it is going to taste when it's done. Sometimes we stuff the chickens and cook them in the steamer.

I like steamer cooking on top of the stove best because we cook the liver, the gizzard, and the heart on top of the stove, then grind them up and add them to the stuffing. If the chickens are going to end up as chicken and dumplings, we put the insides in the pot along with the rest of the chicken, and I can try and sneak my favorite part—the gizzard—out of the pot before any of the other kids get to it. Actually, I'm not sure any of the other kids even like the gizzard because I never asked any of them. After all, whenever kids know somebody else wants something, they always seem to want it too.

There are some other things my mother cooks that everybody likes. One treat is called *ragoût de pattes de cochon,* which is a French term. The *pattes* is "feet" in French, which actually is the bottom of the leg of a pig. Ma browns flour in a frying pan and then adds water to make a paste, which she adds to the legs being cooked in a rather large pot. I'm not sure why this tastes so good. I think she must add other stuff.

Suet pudding is one special treat made for days like Christmas. It is a delicious brown, heavy, raisin-filled dessert that we cook in a one-quart can. We put the can of pudding mixture into a pot of boiling water until the water is within one inch of the can's lid. Boy, the pudding is so good. Ma makes a kind of almost-clear sauce of some kind that we pour over the pudding.

Something else that is very good is milk gravy. First, Ma browns the flour, then she adds milk. We pour the gravy over boiled potatoes. Sometimes she adds something extra good, like meat. That is one of the things Antoinette brags about at school—her mother adds tuna fish and other fancy stuff. She lives on a farm too. I don't know where they get the money for tuna fish. Maybe it's because there are only a couple of kids in her family.

My mother's soups are always good. She starts with a little fat in the pot, then adds tomatoes, then other vegetables. Sometimes there is canned beef, rice, or macaroni in the soup. I'm not sure in what particular order the different things are added into the soup. I guess you can't go wrong with vegetable soup.

20

Cellar ~ Grandma's Refrigerator ~ Cutting Wood

The cellar in our house is quite a wonderful place. When I open the door to go down the open cellar stairs, there is the same smell of dark wet earth that there is in the mysterious forest. On the right-hand side of the stairway is a row of shelves. The top shelves are much shorter than the bottom ones because the shelves are built under the stairs at the front of the house. The space on the shelves is the only place we have to try to keep foods cool.

One time my grandmother Langevin was getting rid of her refrigerator. I feel so bad when my Grandmother Langevin has her favorite children be the only ones who make decisions for her. First come the four Benedictine nuns in St. Marys, Pennsylvania, then comes her youngest son, the smashing-looking Uncle Joe in the navy. Next are the uppity Buffalo relatives, Aunt Clarinda with her kids, and Aunt Mina's kids. Then, last, is Uncle Rod on a farm—and my mother. Somehow, all Grandma's children, except my mother, seem to get into the act of helping her make decisions.

Mom, Dad, and all us kids were waiting to hear about us getting Grandma's refrigerator. Everybody knew about the large number of Patnode kids and that we had no refrigerator. Besides, we live in Ellenburg Center—only a few miles away from Grandma in Ellenburg Corners. She lives almost directly across from the big school that the kids from the three Ellenburgs—Ellenburg Center, Ellenburg Corners, and Ellenburg Depot—are bused to. All Grandma's other children and grandchildren live far away. A couple of months went by, and then Grandma Langevin's old refrigerator just disappeared. I never found out where it went. I think everybody in my family feels bad about that. After all, my mother was the only child of Grandma who had gone down into "The Valley of Death" twelve times to get each of her twelve kids. Grandma should know she deserves something special on earth. I don't know why the church calls having a kid going into "The Valley of Death."

The shelves at the top of the cellar stairs hold a lot of different things. There is a bottle of cod-liver oil on the top shelf. Sometimes Ma tries to get us to take a spoonful. We all try to get out of that one. It tastes so bad. The shelves also hold milk in a milk pail that comes from the barn, jars of pickles and jams that have been opened but not all used up, eggs, and—when we get government give-away—slabs of butter.

The cellar floor is dirt. At the foot of the stairs is the beginning of a three-foot-wide walking space. Across from the stairs is what looks like a six-foot-long old wooden box about two feet high in front and three and one-half feet high in back. It is closed at both ends and has no top or bottom. Halfway up inside is dirt. We use it for winter storage of things like carrots and turnips if, in the fall, anybody gets around to putting garden stuff in there. It also is where we keep bushel baskets of wonderful McIntosh apples.

At the foot of the stairs, all the way up on the right wall, is a little window that sure doesn't let in very much light through all the dust and cobwebs. It is hard enough to try and get the windows washed in the other parts of the house. I'm pretty sure that window washing mostly happened when my mother had hired girls for about the first five kids or so, then, when she kept having more kids, I think we just got too poor. Good people like my mother and father know all about why we are put on this earth. It isn't to have fun. It's to save our souls.

In winter, that little cellar window sometimes doesn't let in any light at all because snow piles up against it. Other times, since it faces north, a fierce howling winter wind manages to blow snow in through the little space at the bottom. There isn't any question about how cold it is outside when some snow is getting into the cellar from the window frame. The big round furnace where we burn chunks of wood and sometimes coal is only seven feet away from that little window. During the winter, we keep the furnace burning all day long and Dad stokes it to burn through most of the night. In the cellar ceiling, over the furnace, is the metal grate in the floor of the dining room that gives out the only heat for the entire renovated west side of the house.

As you come down the cellar stairs, to the left are two shelves—one over the other—which are hung from the rafters. They are about three feet wide and six feet long and run from the stairs to just past the furnace. Here we store glass quart jars of canned chunks of beef, berries, corn, and beans, along with small glass jars of paraffin-sealed currant and crab apple jelly. Under the shelves is the big twelve-foot-long and four-and-one-half-foot-high round water storage tank that holds the water for the kitchen sink, the washroom sink, the washing machine, and the upstairs and downstairs bathrooms.

Under the stairs and between the stairs and the water tank, we store a barrel of salt pork in a salty brine, a five-gallon ceramic crock of pickled cucumbers, and sometimes even a crock of eggs in some kind of brine. Egg storage sure doesn't happen very often because mostly we don't even have enough for everyday use. The stored eggs can only be used for baking. The egg whites turn a sort of slimy white, but they are okay—and better than no eggs for something like a cake.

Past the water tank and the furnace is a pile of wood that has been thrown down the cellar steps from an opening in the front porch. Actually, I consider getting wood into the house mostly my job, except for some of the bigger chunks for the furnace that are much too heavy for me to carry. I expect the other kids would say how much they do of the jobs I tell you I do.

To move wood to the house from the pile stacked next to the road in front of the house, I harness the small horse Kit and lead her to the wagon that I use. Two parallel two-inch-thick wooden poles are attached to the wagon in front. I back Kit between the poles and hitch her to the flat three-and-one-half-foot-by-seven-foot wagon bed. The wagon has four wheels with wooden spokes and metal rims.

When the big logs come out of the forest, they are rolled off the sled onto the ground between the barn and the garage. I told you before about my father cutting the logs and how he got hurt on the big round saw he uses to cut up the logs into chunks. From there, most of the big chunks are split up with an ax in small enough pieces for the kitchen stove and to start a fire in the furnace. We keep some of the pieces in big chunks that we use in the cellar furnace. The bigger chunks are added to keep the fire burning for a lot longer. The furnace door and its insides are big enough to allow pretty big chunks.

Sometimes there isn't a man to put a big chunk of wood in the furnace in the middle of the day when there isn't much heat coming through the dining room grate and the house is getting cold. That's a time when I sure try to find a chunk of wood small enough for me to get from the pile of logs at the bottom of the stairs all the way into the furnace. Only the men are strong enough to move the really big chunks of wood.

Wood that is to be used in the kitchen stove is stacked to dry in cord measures in long rows four feet high. The rows are just north of the dirt road between our main driveway and the hired man's house.

Before I start moving wood, I try and make sure that Ma or Dad will make another kid help me. Sometimes that doesn't work too well because I'll get somebody who's pretty mad at having to help move wood.

I steer Kit to the stacked wood next to the road and load on as much as will stay on the wagon without falling off. From there I steer Kit to the back of the house where there is a hinged, three-foot-square trapdoor that opens into the woodshed. I get the wagon as close as I possibly can to the house with just barely enough room for us to stand between the wagon and the little door. It's pretty hard work, and I don't want to carry the wood any farther than we have to. I say "we" because, by now, Ma or Dad will probably have made one of my sisters help me. We unload the wood into the house. Sam, the only boy older than I, and the oldest one in the family, is already doing a grown man's job somewhere else on the farm.

Over and over again, I load up the wagon as high as I can, then go back to the house to throw the wood through the trapdoor into the woodshed. By the time the wood inside the woodshed gets up to the edge of the bottom of the trapdoor, it is time to go into the woodshed and stack the wood. We stack wood against the far wall going south from the northwest corner for about fifteen feet to the window. When we've stacked one row that is six feet high and fifteen feet long, we start another row in front of the first one.

I can tell the woodshed has been added onto the north side of the house. Inside the woodshed, the north wall used to be part of the outside of the house and still has the same shingles as the rest of the house. There is a door in the woodshed that leads into the house next to the back stairs that go to the second floor. At the base of the same stairs to the left is the door to the first-floor bathroom, and to the right is the entrance to the kitchen.

Back and forth I go with the horse and wagon—load the wood, then toss the wood inside the woodshed, then stack the wood. I have to be careful how we stack the wood. Nobody wants to see the wall of stacked wood come crashing down. What a pickle that would be for the kid whose fault that was. Boy, it sure feels awfully good when the stacks fill all the space except for a little bit of room in front of the hinged door, and I can think about having nice dry wood to burn all winter long.

In front of our house, facing the road, is the opening in the porch that is a large two-sided trapdoor that leads to the five cement steps that go down into the cellar. The trapdoor to the cellar is next to cement steps that go from the driveway to the porch. Under the trapdoor and down the steps is where my father, the hired man, or my brother Sam heaves the big chunks of wood for the furnace. I throw some cordwood down there too. Nobody can start a fire with just a big chunk of wood.

21

Canning Tomatoes ~ Sagging Bed

There are a lot of interesting things in the cellar. In addition to the shelves hanging from rafters over the water tank, in the southwest corner, there is a large, two-by-six-foot, two-level wooden platform that holds about five hundred glass quart jars. Before winter there are about 375 jars of tomatoes on those shelves. Canning tomatoes is almost fun. Somehow, they seem to just appear in bushel baskets on the front porch—big, fat, beautiful, round, red tomatoes that smell so good. After a couple of weeks of canning, and just before the first frost, the tomatoes start getting softer, and a couple already start to spoil, so that is when we really have to rush to finish the job. The kitchen sink is where most of the work is done.

The white ceramic sink is eighteen by thirty inches, and four inches deep. It is under the plywood kitchen cabinets that my big brother Sam built. There is a water faucet swing arm that goes left and right, and a handle to turn the water, hot or cold. There are white enamel-covered metal drain boards on each side of the sink. The drain boards have a slightly raised edge on three sides. The fourth side laps over the side of the sink. The drain boards have ridges in the middle part—something like the ridges in a washboard used for a few clothes when washing them by hand. The ridges on the drain boards are smooth, not as high, and about three times as far apart as those on the washboard.

My brothers joined three homemade plywood cabinets over the kitchen sink that start at the ceiling. Over each drain board the cabinets are about eighteen inch deep and eighteen inches wide by two feet high. They have a shelf in the middle behind a hinged door. The cabinet on the left holds pots and pans, while the cabinet on the right holds chipped enamel tin plates and cups. Of course, the cabinet directly over the sink starts much higher so the kids washing the dishes under it won't bump their heads. I'm pretty tall, so sometimes, if I'm not careful, I bump my head on the cabinet. I think that, of all the chores, dishwashing is the one that causes the most fights among us kids. "I washed them last." "You did not, I did." "Well I dried them, and now it's somebody else's turn."

I'll bet at least half of the chipped edges on our metal dishes are because of a mad kid. The chipped, blue gray, enamel metal dishes are so ugly—especially when I think about Mrs. Smith's or my grandmother's nice china dishes. I sure am embarrassed when somebody not in our Sam Patnode family can see our awful dishes.

Then there is the youngest kid. When she got old enough, we would ask Ma, "Why isn't Bernadette ever made to wash the dishes?" My mother's response was, "There are enough big girls to do it," and she would tell us which one of the big girls is going to do what. And that, of course, starts all the arguments all over again. My poor mother—with all those kids and all that arguing, then having to do what the Catholic Church says about everything, it's no wonder she seems so unhappy most of the time.

When we can tomatoes, the first thing we do is get water boiling on the kitchen stove. Then we fill a large pot with tomatoes and bring the pot to the kitchen sink. We pour the boiling water from the stove over the tomatoes until they are covered. The tomatoes have to stay in very hot water for only a couple of minutes. Next, we drain the water off into the sink. Of course, in the meantime, there has to be more water getting hot on the stove for the next batch. The hot water bath sure makes the tomatoes easy to peel. On the left drain board, we set out the empty glass quart jars.

After paring a bit off where the stem was, and peeling the tomatoes, we pack them whole into the glass jars. When the tomatoes reach the top, we push them down until the tomato juice from the tomatoes fills any empty spaces. Sometimes we have to cut a tomato in half to get the jar filled to just the right height—half an inch from the top. Next, we put a thin, flat rubber ring around the little glass ledge at the top of the jar. This acts as a seal. We have to be very careful not to leave too much air in the jar and to make sure not to leave seeds or any pieces of tomato on the rubber ring. Finally, we put the glass lid on the jar and tighten one-half of the metal "bail," which is a two-piece metal clamp that holds the glass lid on tight during the steaming process. When the jars are put into the two-shelf steamer on top of the stove, there can't be anything that might let air back into the jar during its long sealing steam bath. It is so important to have canned food to eat during the bitter cold winters.

The garden we plant in the spring may also give us other things to can like corn, string beans, peas, and even beets, which nobody seems to like very much. Usually it seems as if the garden probably won't be cared for enough to give us very much for canning. Weeding never seems to get done as the weeds get pretty high late in the season. In the middle of April, when there is still a lot of snow on the ground, I try to start tomato plants from seeds in a flat wooden box filled with dirt. I put the box on a wooden crate in front of a small south-facing, second-floor window in a bedroom that sometimes is my bedroom.

The room has a regular-size bed against the north wall that is used by two kids. The bed sags toward the middle, so when I sleep on that bed I always sleep on my stomach to make sure I won't have a homely rounded back when I grow up. Part of the room is actually a hall. In the middle of the room is an opening the size of a door where there is a little step up that goes to the newer part of the house with its hardwood floors. On the other side of the room is an opening the size of a door that goes to the rest of the older part of the house.

There is a flight of stairs at each end of the house, but the one upstairs bathroom is in the old part of the house, so there sure are many trips through the hall part of the room in the middle of the house. Sometimes the kids who sleep in the double bed try to get a little privacy by rigging up a sheet curtain on wire from one side of the room to the other side. On the small window side of the room is a small dresser with a mirror. On the other side of the wall is the bathroom sink.

In that same middle room, against the wall between the window and the opening to the newer part of the house, is a cot. Sometimes that gets to be my bed. The head part is on the wall next to the small window. The cot has a flat open metal spring bottom on metal legs that holds a straw-filled mattress. When it has just been filled, it is fat and puffed up. With just a heavy ticking cover holding the straw, not only is it pretty bumpy, but if one of the straws is kind of stiff, it pokes at me right through the cover. After a while, the straw gets packed down, but that is one place where none of us kids likes to sleep. Of course, it has to be a girl because boys and girls can't sleep in the same room, and there are already girls in the double bed in the same room. The whole time, Sam, my oldest brother, has a wonderful small bedroom on the first floor all to himself. It has a single bed, a dresser, and its very own small closet that even has shelves, although Ma's things pretty much take up the whole closet. Sam doesn't have that many things. Actually, I don't think anybody even thinks of that closet as Sam's because it holds so many of Ma's things.

I forgot to tell you a while back about a very serious thing that happened when Sam had an accident and his big toe had to be got cut off. There was such worrying. There he was, in bed with the infection spreading and in such danger of maybe losing his whole leg, and my mother and father not knowing what to do with the cut-off toe because every part of a Catholic's body is holy—especially if the person does all the things our mother and father make us do, like mass and confession and saying so many prayers.

Should they ask the priest at St. Edmund's Church in Ellenburg Corner, Father Boyer, if the holy toe could be buried someplace near my grandmother and grandfather's grave in back of the St. Edmund's Church? It was a big problem. My mother and father sure weren't hollering when they were talking about that toe. That question of what to do was whispered about for days. I never did find out what they did with Sam's toe, but I suspect they buried it in holy ground next to my grandparents' burial plot in back of Saint Edmund's Church when nobody was looking.

22

Playhouse ~ Garden ~ GLF

Our garden is planted in one of two places, either in back of the barn or in back of the playhouse Dad built for us. The playhouse is about thirty feet from the southeast corner of our farmhouse—the side where there is an open porch and where I try to grow morning glories on twine. Our playhouse is very special. No other kids at school—not even the rich city kids—have anything like that. My dad built it long before I can remember. I am the fifth kid. By the time I came along, Dad was awfully busy with what must have been even more chores than before.

The playhouse is about twelve by fifteen feet. The walls are wooden planks about three-fourths of an inch thick and ten inches wide, and cover a frame of two-by-fours. There is a window and door opening cut out in the wall that faces the house. Just inside the doorway is a stairway that leads to a very little attic. The slanting roof meets the floor of the attic on two sides. Even the little attic has a floor we can walk on, and, in the middle, we can stand up straight. Actually, we don't get to use the playhouse very much. The few times we are free from farm or house chores or prayers, we usually find some more fun things to do. Summertime is for playing ball if we can find a bat and one of the tennis balls Aunt Clarinda sent. Sometimes we play in the hay in the barn, or we play Chinese checkers in the house. Fun times sure don't happen very often.

When it gets warm enough to start planting the garden, it is as if the entire cold, and often unfriendly and brutal outdoors, turns into such a wonderful and beautiful place. The smell of freshly turned earth, small pink roses, and the flowering crab apple trees all come together to once more welcome me in their embrace. First, we turn over the earth in the garden patch with a horse-drawn harrow. The harrow has teeth that are dragged over the ground. They break up the soil that has become packed down with the winter weather of bitter cold with its endless piles of windblown snow. The next thing that either a kid or my mother or father does is to use a hoe—a long-handled tool with a three-by-five-inch flat blade at the end to chop up any clumps of dirt, then go back and forth with the hoe until the dirt is fairly smooth. This is the one time of the year that my mother seems to be kind of happy.

The seeds for the garden usually come from a feed store called the GLF in Ellenburg Depot. I don't get to see the inside of the store very often, but I sure like it when I do. There are lots of different things for sale in the store. There are hundreds of burlap bags of feed that fill up most of a very large storage area. The bags are filled with different kinds of grains like oats and wheat that farmers use mostly for animals like horses, cows, sheep, pigs, and chickens. They are laid flat and stacked up one on top of the other in rows almost to the ceiling—except for the front row where the grain to sell is taken from. Often at the open, big sliding doors of the storage part of the store, we can watch men unloading from a big delivery truck, or we can see a farmer loading bags in the back of his truck or wagon.

The seed part of the store is where we find things like garden tools, rakes, pitchforks, shovels, salt blocks, barn and garden gloves, and even things like cement and some animal medication. It's also where we buy vegetable and flower seeds. The air carries some dust from the dried and ground-up plant seeds that make up animal feed. I sure like the smell of the store where the bags of feed give off the same kind of earthy scent we breathe when we thresh the oats at our farm. (That's when the plant stalk, which is called straw, is separated from the grain by a big piece of farm machinery, which blows the straw into an opening in the second floor of the old eastern end of the barn, and feeds the oat grain into burlap bags.)

We usually have pumpkin seeds from last year's pumpkins if somebody remembers to put the seeds aside when they cook the pumpkins in the fall. If we've all forgotten, we need to buy pumpkin seeds along with whatever other seeds we are going to plant. Pumpkin seeds are planted among the corn; I'm not sure why. String beans, peas, carrots, turnips, radishes, and lettuce make up the rest of the planting. Whenever I can, I try to get my parents to order Shumway seeds from the catalog. The man who heads up our 4H Club says they are the best, and he is a teacher. Besides, I'm sure they have to be better than what we could buy at grumpy, not-talking Uncle Ed's store at Ellenburg Center, or even at the GLF that has all kinds of farm supplies.

The patch of land that is made ready for planting is about twenty-five feet by seventy-five feet. A kid or my mother puts a little stick in the ground on the twenty-five-foot end, then ties a piece of twine to the stick and walks with the twine the seventy-five feet to the other end of the row to tie the twine to a stick on that end. It seems to me that Ma and I are the only ones that do a pretty good job of making a straight row. Ma does a lot of this stuff even though she doesn't do any of the regular farm chores like milking cows and feeding the farm animals, except sometimes she feeds the chickens. Maybe I should keep in mind all the things she has to do in the house like making meals and taking care of the little kids.

The rows have to be far enough apart that later on somebody can walk between the rows to weed and, later, harvest the vegetables. First we mark row after row with string, then we make a little valley along the string with the hoe to put the seeds into. Putting seeds into the little valley has to be done very carefully because some seeds look like little specks and have to be sprinkled sparingly, and some are large enough to be dropped one by one. We put the empty seed packets on the stick at the end of the row so we know what's planted, and then we use the hoe to cover the seeds. We have to be careful not to put too much dirt on top of the seeds or they won't grow at all—especially the very little seeds.

If only spring could last forever, with the smell of the earth just turned, the temperature getting warmer outside, the heat of the sun so cozy and not too hot the way it is in July and August, the obvious joy of animals exhibiting wild abandon on their release outside from their winter jails. I think it's probably a wonderful feeling for everything and everybody. Even the kids in my family don't seem to fight very much in the spring.

Radishes are the first garden planting to pop out their little green leaves. I always try to be the first to sneak into the garden to pull out the little green radish plant with its tiny pink radish, but another kid often gets there before I do. The first radishes and the first carrots in early spring are very small and have very little color. I can't take them anywhere to wash them; somebody might see me. But who can wait? So I brush off the dirt as best I can and even that tiny first taste is so wonderful. I think Ma probably knows that we kids do that, but how can she say anything if there isn't another kid who sees the snitching and tells her?

For the first few weeks, the garden looks like a picture-book garden: the seeds are ahead of the weeds, and all the rows of tiny different green shapes and sizes look so orderly—like little soldiers with great promise. There are little corn stalks with tiny green pumpkin leaves at their feet, whispery carrot tops, low, bunchy radish leaves, small pea vines already knowing they have to climb—all telling of things to come.

Boy, it sure isn't long before weeds try their best to take over and give the vegetables a big fight for space. The weeds that grow the fastest and are the strongest and have the biggest roots are called pig weeds, but, of course, there are lots of other weeds. I have barn chores to do. When will one of my sisters, who has no barn chores, be told by my mother to do the weeding? The time never seems to come, and the weeds keep getting bigger and taller. Of course, the longer the weeds go without being pulled, the worse it is for the vegetables. It just doesn't seem fair—all the careful preparation and planting and then the garden gets almost no care. I don't know what my older sisters are doing. Maybe they might be taking care of some of the younger ones or whatever, but they sure don't seem to do very much because the house always looks like such a mess.

I sure know when my special jobs have to be done both in the summer and in the winter. In the summer I go on horseback to get the cows out of the day pasture. I'm sure not complaining about that. I love everything about the pastures and fields, the horse I ride, the ever-changing woods, the smells, and the plants, trees, rocks, and the wild animals. I also rake the freshly cut hay and help with milking, feeding animals, and all the things that have to be done on a very busy farm.

Most of the time, nobody pulls out the weeds, and they just keep growing. I suppose my mother tries to get one kid or another out there to weed. I sure wish I could make my older sisters take care of the garden. Sometimes the weeds get as tall as the vegetables! Every once in a while, I can't stand it any more, and, after a long day of other chores, I go out and do some weeding.

Even with a lot of weeds growing, the garden is nice to have. We don't get any fresh vegetables in the wintertime. Any vegetables we have, except for the tomatoes and the potatoes from our own field, come from the garden. Actually, there aren't too many of the glass jars that are filled with canned vegetables from our garden because there are all us kids to feed in summer as well as in winter. If there is anything left to can in the summertime, it is most likely to be corn or green beans. When we can corn, first we have to cut the corn off the cob, and then we pack it into quart jars and put them into the steamer for a certain length of time. It seems to take forever to cut enough corn off the cob to fill even one quart jar.

23

Sugarhouse ~ Maple Syrup ~ Blackberries

In the fields and pastures of our Ellenburg Center, New York, three-hundred-acre farm there are a lot of rocks—from very big to very small. The farm is on the northern edge of the Adirondack Mountains. The day pasture starts a quarter mile in back of the barn at the foot and on the north side of our small mountain. There is a little trickling stream at the base of the mountain. Along its banks is eight-foot-high wild brush. The pasture continues up the mountain until the mountain and the sky meet.

Before we get to the beautiful woods, which are more than halfway up the mountain, we pass, scattered about, many gray, scraggly-looking, unevenly shaped rocks as much as three feet high. Moss, in various mixed shades of light green, gray, and brown, clings to the sides of most of the rocks. Among the rocks and the sparse grass are tree stumps in various stages of decay. The sugarhouse, which is used for making maple syrup from the nearby maple trees, is partway up the mountain.

I can tell about how long ago a tree has been cut down by how rotten a tree stump is. Of course, where my father has cut down trees for our kitchen stove and the furnace, the stumps look as if they have been more recently mortally wounded. I like to think about how beautiful the mountain must have looked when all the ugly stumps were tall maple trees giving shade in their green glory in the summer and making so many people happy with wonderful maple syrup in the spring and summer. Sometimes, if the sap run is very good because the weather is just right, the maple sugar we harvest might even last into the following winter. There is no other taste that has the same combination of earth, sky, and sweet love as maple syrup.

East of the sugarhouse is a barbed wire fence that runs up the side of the mountain. The fence starts at the little stream and goes all the way up the mountain, past the eastern side of the sugar house, and the mysterious forest of the day pasture, to the fenced southernmost unproductive hayfields. When I ride Kit in the day pasture to get the cows for evening milking, it sure makes finding the cows easier that the cows can't drift down to the night pasture, which is on the other side of the barbed wire fence.

The night pasture doesn't have very much grass. It's almost flat, and all that I can see from the top of the mountain in the day pasture is rocks of all sizes. Since cows don't graze during the darkness of the night, not much grass is all right. All the rocks and the scanty vegetation of the night pasture are friendly for the few little scraggly low blueberry bushes that grow there. There never are very many blueberries, but, once in a while, one of us manages to pick a cup of blueberries to bring home so that someone can make frosting for a cake. Any kind of berries, a cup of sugar, and one egg white beaten to a fluffy mix sure makes tasty frosting for a white cake.

There is a place on some government land near one of the Ellenburgs where, every few years, there are big fat blueberries on bushes about three feet high for people who can find them and be brave enough to not be too worried about what somebody might say if they are seen. We picked there only a couple of times. I sure would have gone every year, but there isn't any way to find the spot or to get there without a big person.

Very early in springtime, when there is still snow on the ground, it's time to start preparing to make maple syrup. The first thing that my father and a hired man or my brother Sam do is go to our stand of maple trees near the top of our little mountain and drill holes in them—about three and one-half feet off the ground. Next they pound into the hole a round metal spout that is about three inches long and has an X-cut open into the part that goes into the tree. The outside end of the spout has a little wire hanger where we hang a bucket. The sap runs out into the bucket. Sometimes, if the tree is very big, the men put two, and sometimes even three, buckets on the same tree.

I don't know how my father knows when to start tapping maple trees, as there will still be snow on the ground for most of the short season of making maple syrup, and there isn't a special day that he starts. I always wonder that, just maybe, trees that are cut down or drilled like the maples are hurt at least a little bit like people. I wish I could protect everything I love. The maple trees give us that wonderful candylike maple syrup and shade in the summer besides looking so pretty.

To start many farm chores, first my father hitches up our working team of horses. I am calling those two horses the working team because we always have three horses. First, there is "my Kit." I like to call her that because she is the horse I ride for going after the cows for milking, for raking the hay, hauling firewood, and for hitching to the cutter in winter. The working team used to be Queen, and the horse we called "old Tom," a reddish-colored horse. But Tom has now been replaced with wild, beautiful, huge Ned. When I was a very little kid, Queen probably was a bit gray, but now she is mostly white. Sometimes she falls down when she seems to be asleep. When horses fall down, they make a lot more noise than they do when they lie down on purpose. Sometimes horses sleep standing up and sometimes they sleep lying down. It sure seems funny to think of them sleeping when they are standing up.

My father or my brother drives our team of horses pulling a sleigh from the barn and up the mountain to the sugar bush. There, they put a tank on the sleigh for collecting the sap from the trees. While one man drives the horses, the other man and the kids keep going back and forth taking the buckets off the trees, emptying them into the tank on the sled, then replacing the empty bucket on the tree and going on to the next full bucket. When the buckets are almost filled to the top, they sure do get heavy.

In the sugarhouse, there is a very long, flat, rather thin metal pan about ten by three feet and ten inches deep. It is suspended about two feet off the ground. After the sap from the maple trees is poured inside the pan, we build a fire underneath. The sap of a maple tree looks like water that is just a little bit cloudy. It has only a little bit of a sweet taste. We store the empty buckets in the low-roofed second floor of the sugarhouse, ready for the next year. In the middle of the roof there is an opening that is raised about a foot and has its own little roof. This is where the steam escapes out of the sugarhouse when we are boiling down the sap into syrup.

What a wonderful time of year maple sugaring is. I don't know why the other kids don't seem to love it as much as I do. The gathering of sap and getting it to the sugarhouse for boiling down to that oh-so-tasty maple syrup is one of the very best times of the year.

During the boiling process, Dad has to be very careful that, when the sap starts to thicken and bubble up, it doesn't keep right on rising and bubble over the edges of the long pan. He has to make sure that he keeps a little piece of fatty pork on a string hanging over the boiling sap. When the hot syrupy bubbles reach the fat, a little bit of fat melts, and, right away, down go the bubbles. Sometimes the sun makes a few bare spots in the snow, and the earthy smell of newly exposed soil mingles with that of boiling sap.

There is one night that stands out as one of those times that makes me know how much my father loves us. There were other kids around, but nobody else could have been as happy as I was. That special night was near the sugarhouse on the side of the mountain with my treasured maple trees just a little higher up. The moon lighted the night into a fairyland of sparkling white snow and twinkling stars. The biggest show-offs were the Big Dipper, the Little Dipper, and the North Star, which stood out in their special majesty, with all the others crowding the picture into nighttime magic.

I don't think there will ever be a time or place more perfect. Dad made a big fire over which he put a pot of maple syrup to thicken till it was perfect for putting on snow—it has to be perfect, so that, when you pour it onto the snow, it hardens on top and doesn't just sink in. While the maple syrup boiled, Dad kept testing it until it was thick enough. Then he ladled out a generous amount onto the snow. We kids grabbed little sticks we had found lying around and scrambled to pick up the strings of taffylike candy. When did my father ever find time for doing something so fancy? Could it be just a dream even if it's so real to me? Or could it be that I so much wanted it that it became real to me? Sometimes I wonder.

Maple syrup never seems to even last all the way through the summer. One time, when we were up in the sugar bush collecting sap, out of the corner of my eye I saw a chipmunk come out of a tree. I had never seen one at this time of the year, and I so much wanted to pet it. I watched it go back into a hole in the tree. Dad said I'd better not touch it because it might bite. Well, of course, I put my hand where the chipmunk had gone back in. I wanted to get that little guy out of there—maybe I could make a pet out of it. I sure let it go in a hurry when it bit me.

Our neighbor George Smith's property borders our property from our barn to the middle of the mountain. There the boundary between our properties makes a ninety degree turn to the right, enlarging our day pastureland higher up the mountain on the south side. A large portion of our day pasture is south of George Smith's, which is the flatter top part of the mountain where there are a lot of different kinds of brush; a few evergreen trees; some rocks partially covered by shrunken, clingy moss; and uneven, poor-looking earth with scanty, scattered, dried-looking, brownish green grass.

Brush is growth of about three to eight feet tall of scraggly bush that combines in clumps of different sizes from several feet to fifteen or twenty feet across. In some places, the brush is so thick that we have to keep finding another way to keep walking. Or there can be many fewer bushes among rocky dirt and dried-up grass and weeds. Once in a while, there is a tree that might end up being a Christmas tree.

In the middle, or mixed in with the other brush, is where the blackberry bushes are. I don't know why, but some years, even if it doesn't rain too much or not enough, there aren't many blackberries. Every once in a while, though, there are enough blackberries to fill a few buckets, and we end up canning quart jars of blackberries, which we store on a shelf in the cellar next to the tomatoes. That's when we may even have some extra for making a couple of delicious blackberry pies.

Actually, we kids, and sometimes Ma, if there might be a lot of berries, each get something as big as a quart can to fill. When our one-quart can is full, we find whoever is carrying the twelve-quart milk pail brought along by the biggest kid among us. We all dump our berries into the big pail and keep trying to find more berries. When there are that many blackberries, I thank God. The bad part, of course, is all the thorns on the bushes. The fattest berries always seem to be the hardest ones to reach, and require getting past the biggest and longest thorns. Getting stuck and scratched with thorns is sure worth the smell and taste of wonderful blackberry pie, especially when, every once in a while, we have enough left over so we have a few quart jars of blackberries as a treat during the so very cold winter.

All Dressed Up at Gagniers' House

Joe   Rose   Marie   Mom   Jeannette   Dad   Sam Jr.   Rita   Theresa
                               Gemma   Marguerite

Edgar Gagnier Family

The Edgar Gagnier family of Chuorbusco, NY,
were potato farmers, and possibly bootleggers!

Here are all the girls in the Sam and Jeannette
Patnode family of twelve children, except for Marie.
The playhouse that their Dad built is in the background.

Dad

(being held)   Rita
Gemma   Rose   Bernie   Theresa
Jeannette   Marguerite

Here are all the boys in the Sam and Jeannette Patnode
family of twelve children.

Sam, Joe, Raymond, Paul

Rose holds a horse next to the hay wagon. Raymond,
Paul, and Marguerite stand on the front of the wagon,
while baby Bernadette tries to join them.

(on hayrack)
Raymond Paul
        Marguerite
Bernadette

Rose
(holding horse reigns)

Theresa and Sam, Junior, take a ride on a horse.

Theresa stands with her father in front of the family car on the day of her First Communion.

The Patnode children play at being a priest and nuns. Diapers serve as headdresses. The hired man's house is in the background with wood stacked in cords next to it. At the right of the picture is more wood stacked in cords next to the East-West dirt road.

Sam   Marie   Rita
    Gemma   Theresa Rose

St. Edmund's Catholic Church was built
in the 1880s in Ellenburg Corners, New
York. This picture is of the left isle
facing Mother Mary's altar, which is in
the foreground.

This is the inside St. Edmund's Catholic Church as
seen from the choir loft.

Theresa's

First

Communion

                Marie   Rita
        Rose   Sam Jr.   Theresa

All dressed for winter cold

Sam, Marie, Rita, Theresa, Rose

Theresa's family attended
St. Edmund's Catholic
Church in Ellenburg, New
York.

Old St. Edmund's Church Hall was built at the turn
of the twentieth century. Horses were stabled on
the ground floor during church services and functions,
and church functions were held on the second floor.

Souvenir of Theresa's First Holy Communion

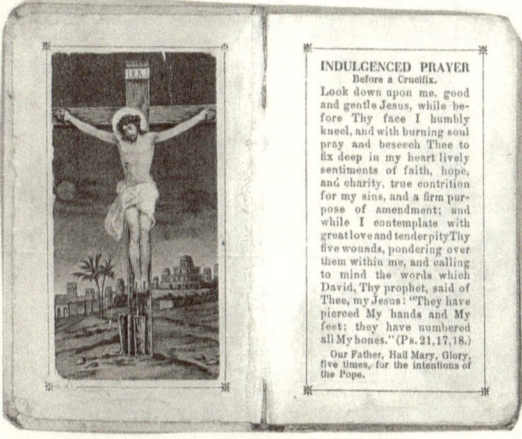

INDULGENCED PRAYER
Before a Crucifix.

Look down upon me, good and gentle Jesus, while before Thy face I humbly kneel, and with burning soul pray and beseech Thee to fix deep in my heart lively sentiments of faith, hope, and charity, true contrition for my sins, and a firm purpose of amendment; and while I contemplate with great love and tender pity Thy five wounds, pondering over them within me, and calling to mind the words which David, Thy prophet, said of Thee, my Jesus: "They have pierced My hands and My feet; they have numbered all My bones." (Ps. 21, 17, 18.)

Our Father, Hail Mary, Glory, five times, for the intentions of the Pope.

Souvenir of
my first holy
communion

Theresa Patnode
Ellenburg Corners
N. Y.
St. Edmund's
church
Father Boyer
priest
July 14, 1937

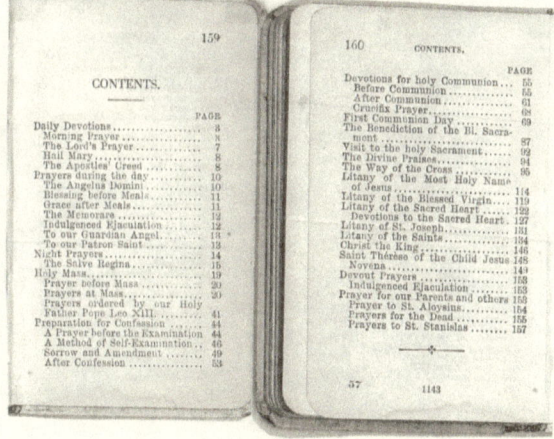

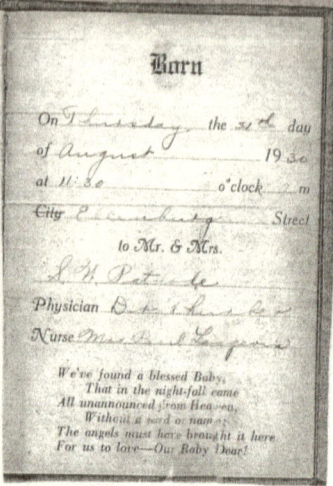

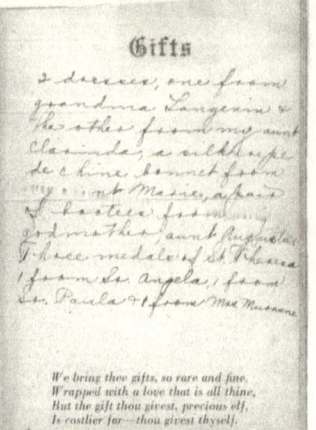

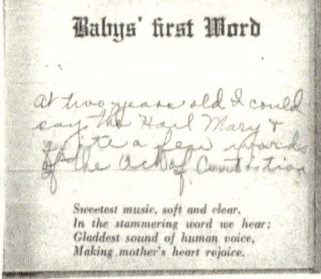

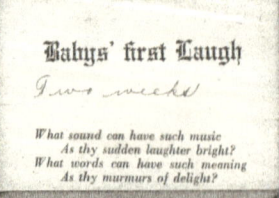

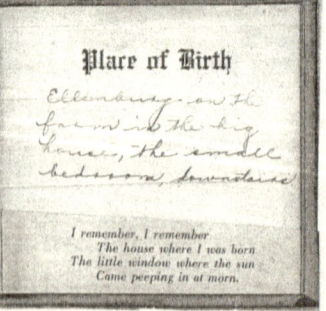

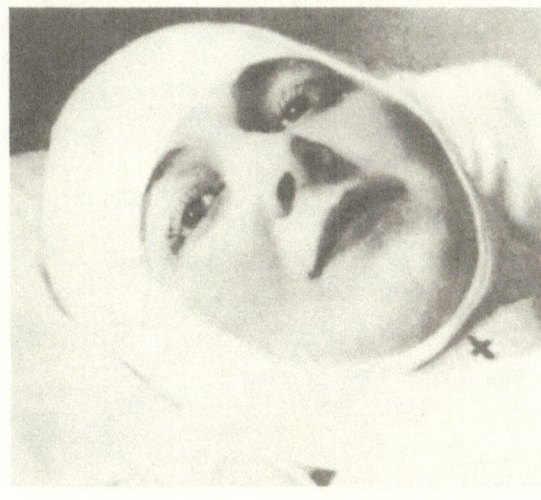

Marie Rose Ferron, known as "Little Rose," was a stigmatized ecstatic, a visionary, and a mystic. She lived in Woonsocket, Rhode Island, and died in 1936 at the age of 33.

Father Onesime Boyer, pastor at St. Edmund's Church in Ellenburg, NY, from 1914 to 1942, wrote a book about Little Rose Ferron entitled She Wears a Crown of Thorns.

Theresa's brother Raymond Patnode was baptized
by Rev O.A. Boyer with sponsors J.B. Ferron and
Delinia Ferron, parents of Marie Rose Ferron also
known as "Little Rose."

Certificate of Baptism

St. Edmund's Church
ELLENBURG, NEW YORK

⇥ This is to Certify ⇤

That *Raymond Joseph Augustine Patnode*

Child of *Samuel Patnode*

and *Jeannette Langevin*

born in *Ellenburg, New York*
(CITY) (STATE)

on the *28th* day of *May* 19 *38*

was

Baptized

on the *4th* day of *June* 19 *38*

According to the Rite of the Roman Catholic Church

by the Rev. *O. A. Boyer*

the Sponsors being { *J.B. Ferron*
Delima Ferron }

as appears from the Baptismal Register of this Church.

Dated *Feb. 13, 1965*

E. J. Faucher
Pastor

No. 314   F. J. REMEY CO., Inc.   MINEOLA, N.Y.

Miss Katie E. White
Teacher at Ellenburg
Depot High School

Sam Patnode dated Katie for eighteen years before marrying Jeannette Langevin. She organized Court Little Rose No. 1300 Catholic Daughters of the Americas in St. Edmund's Parish in 1938 which is active to this day.

St Theresa
of the Child Jesus
July 1896

also
known as
Little flower

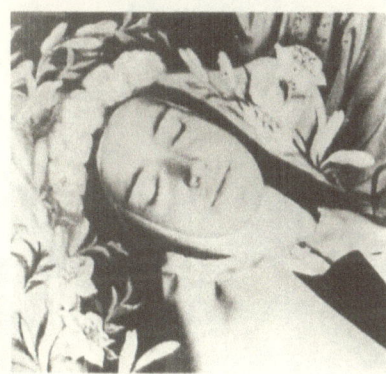

*je ne meurs pas.
j'entre dans la vie*

Uncle
William E. Patnode

This is the store of George O'Connor and
William Patnode. When the Patnode children
visited, Uncle Bill never spoke to them.

Shopping trip to O'Connor and Patnode Store

George O'Connor stands behind the counter
in the store he owned with Theresa's Uncle Bill.

UNITED STATES OF AMERICA
OFFICE OF PRICE ADMINISTRATION

N⁰ 155128-FB

WAR RATION BOOK No. 3

Void if altered

Identification of person to whom issued: PRINT IN FULL

Margaret M. Saper
(First name)   (Middle name)   (Last name)

Street number or rural route ....

City or post office .... State ....

AGE	SEX	WEIGHT Lbs.	HEIGHT Ft. In.	OCCUPATION

SIGNATURE ....
(Person to whom book is issued. If such person is unable to sign because of age or incapacity, another may sign in his behalf.)

WARNING

This book is the property of the United States Government. It is unlawful to sell it to any other person, or to use it or permit anyone else to use it, except to obtain rationed goods in accordance with regulations of the Office of Price Administration. Any person who finds a lost War Ration Book must return it to the War Price and Rationing Board which issued it. Persons who violate rationing regulations are subject to $10,000 fine or imprisonment, or both.

LOCAL BOARD ACTION

Issued by ....
(Local board number)   (Date)

Street address ....

City .... State ....

(Signature of issuing officer)

OPA Form No. R-130.

War Ration Book No. 3

Office of Price Administration

Front

Warning

This book is the property of the United States Government. It is unlawful to sell it to any other person, or to use it or permit anyone else to use it, except to obtain rationed goods in accordance with regulations of the Office of Price Administration. Any person who finds a lost War Ration Book must return it to the War Price and Rationing Board which issued it. Persons who violate rationing regulations are subject to $10,000 fine or imprisonment, or both.

OPA Form No. R-130.

Rationing Books first issued January 1940

Back

Instructions

1. This book is valuable. Do not lose it.
2. Each stamp authorizes you to purchase rationed goods in the quantities and at the times designated by the Office of Price Administration. Without the stamps you will be unable to purchase those goods.
3. Detailed instructions concerning the use of the book and the stamps will be issued from time to time. Watch for those instructions so that you will know how to use your book and stamps. Your Local War Price and Rationing Board can give you full information.
4. Do not throw this book away when all of the stamps have been used, or when the time for their use has expired. You may be required to present this book when you apply for subsequent books.

Rationing is a vital part of your country's war effort. Any attempt to violate the rules is an effort to deny someone his share and will create hardship and discontent.

This book is your Government's assurance of your right to buy your fair share of certain goods made scarce by war. Price ceilings have also been established for your protection. Dealers must post these prices conspicuously. Don't pay more.

Give your whole support to rationing and thereby conserve our vital goods. Be guided by the rule:

*"If you don't need it, **DON'T BUY IT**."*

Return to the Ration Book Index

24

Apples ~ Potatoes ~ Uncle Bill's Store

Between the house and the two acres where we plant our potatoes is a little orchard of three apple trees and five crab apple trees. Some of the trees have much better and more apples than others. A little McIntosh apple tree all the way in the back is the best one of all. Of course, some years are a lot better than others for good apples. There can be too much rain, or not enough—or the hated invasion of caterpillars.

Every spring brings out rather round, irregularly shaped caterpillar nests about the size of a softball. They appear on trees and bushes from about four feet from the ground to way up high. The nests look like very fragile, thin balls of dirty, grayish white cotton with caterpillars crawling all over it. My father burns the nests when they come out in the spring. He winds a couple of oil-soaked rags around the end of a long stick. When he gets to the caterpillar nests, he sets the rags on fire and cooks them alive. Sometimes he doesn't get to the caterpillar job because there are too many more important things to do.

One time, I climbed the McIntosh apple tree to watch the priest from St. Edmund's Church, Father Mallett, land his one-engine plane in the hayfield in back of our house. At that time of the year, the hay in the field wasn't very high. I didn't discover the darn caterpillars on me till I went upstairs to change clothes. I sure made plenty of noise when I felt them crawling on me.

Besides caterpillars, there are other kinds of insects that hurt trees. So, if we don't spray the trees in the spring, there probably won't be very many good apples. With all the other chores like milking cows and bringing in crops to the barn, the apple trees don't get sprayed very often. A lot of times worms end up inside the apples before we get to them.

A crab apple is much smaller than a regular apple. They are about one-fifth the size of our McIntosh apples, are a mixed color of rusty orange red, and are very hard and sour. Ma sometimes cans them in half-quart or quart glass jars. Actually, they aren't good for making pies. Most of the kids don't like them straight from the tree or canned. They are on the sour side for a dessert, but they do make good jelly.

Mostly the apples we get to eat are McIntosh that we buy at the store. Dad brings them back from his Ellenburg Center milk delivery route. I expect they come from Uncle Bill Patnode's store, as his store is the one that sells more things than any other store in Ellenburg Center. There is only one other store, which is across the street from his store. The other store sells mostly things like clothes for women and kids, yarn, sewing notions, and material by the yard.

Uncle Bill's store is quite wonderful, even though he never gives us a single thing—not even one small piece of candy, and he never talks to any of us. As you enter the store, on the right-hand side is a glass-covered case full of different kinds of yummy-looking candy. On the floor in front of that case are uncovered, two-foot-square, wooden, boxlike containers slanted forward to make what's inside easier to see. The boxes are in a row, one right next to the other. They hold things like potatoes, turnips, and beans.

Important things like one-hundred-pound bags of flour and twenty-five-pound bags of sugar are kept in the back room of Uncle Bill's store. Other things in the back room are oil lanterns, lamps, snow shovels, salt blocks, garden tools, brooms, mops, and pails. There is something kind of sad about the one-hundred-pound bags of flour. We kids hear about things like this from grown-ups talking to each other. A couple of the wives of some of the farmers who live farther up our dirt road never leave their farmhouses except for one trip a year to get things like the bags of flour and sugar.

Across the aisle, and taking up a lot of space in the middle of the store, are some enclosed glass cases of things like watches, pens, hair decorations, and fancy handkerchiefs. In spring and summer, a wire stand of vegetable and flower seeds sits on top of the case. On the other side of the glass case are flat wooden boxes a few inches deep on wooden legs as well as tables where you can find things like candles, woolen mittens, scarves, woolen tuques (knitted caps), woolen and cotton socks, as well as all kinds of underwear, long johns, and bloomers. On the back and side walls and in the front windows are things like coveralls and red, green, and plaid flannel shirts.

The long johns my father buys have long arms and legs with buttons down the front and a place in the back that, when spread apart, provides … well, convenience. Of course we can't ever be caught laughing about those kinds of funny things even when there isn't anybody in the long johns. The picture of frozen long john underwear that is put over the furnace to dry is pretty funny. No matter how they are put on the wooden bars of the clothes dryer, the arms and legs are always sticking out some way or other until they thaw a little and then an leg or arm falls down.

We plant potatoes in a field in back of the apple trees. The rows run from north to south for about two hundred feet, and the planting stretches about one hundred fifty feet wide. First, we have to turn the dirt over, then we make trenches, leaving enough space between them so that, when weeds start to grow, a horse pulling what looks like a small plow can be steered between the rows.

In the fall, by the time we finish storing potatoes in the cellar, there is usually a four-foot-high mound of them in the northwest corner. They are not stored in bushel baskets—just dumped on the dirt floor. Sometimes we use our own potatoes for planting but, often, by the time it's time to plant potatoes in June, we will have eaten most of the pile of potatoes during the winter. Besides that, by the time May comes around, the potatoes on the bottom of the pile will have started to sprout. The potato sprout shoots sometimes get as long as seven or eight inches, and the potato will have gotten quite shrunken and wrinkled and no good for planting.

We plant potatoes by dropping about seven to ten pieces of potato in batches every twenty to twenty-four inches along the length of the trench. Then somebody with a hoe follows and covers the potato pieces with dirt. During the time of planting, there is something so nice about everything—the smell of the earth and the sight of all the neat, long, raised rows, and no weeds! Then in a couple of weeks out come little green potato plants peeking out of the brown earth. Soon Dad will be fighting to protect the plants from potato bugs.

To fight potato bugs, my father uses a special tank with attachments. It holds two to three gallons of water. When the darn bugs start to eat the leaves on the potato plants, Dad unscrews the top on the tank and puts in a powder that kills potato bugs. Then he adds water. The water turns a milky white. Then he straps the tank onto his back. The cover of the tank has a three-foot-long little hose at the end of which is a hollow metal rod with a spring handle. This is what my dad uses to squirt the bug poison on the potato plants. Sometimes, if he doesn't get to the plants in time, the potato bugs sure have a lot of good potato leaf meals.

If it rains too much, I hear my father worrying not only about the hay and the oats, but also about the potatoes, especially since in our family there isn't a day when we don't have potatoes to eat for at least one meal. Mostly we cook them by peeling and boiling them. Sometimes, if there is enough time before people come to the table to eat, we mash them. Baking them doesn't happen very often. I think that has something to do with the fact that it takes longer. Another reason might be that it seems as if, when they are baked, whenever dinner is supposed to be ready, either the potatoes, when stuck with a fork, seem almost raw or, if dinner is a little later, they may very well be burned. Any potatoes left over get fried for the next meal.

My mother complained to my dad for what seemed like years. She wanted to have dinner after rather than before the evening chores of milking and feeding the animals. Having dinner after chores made dinnertime somewhere between six thirty and seven o'clock, so you can imagine, with her trying to cook and get kids to help, she wasn't very happy. Well, finally Dad said all right, we would have dinner before the evening chores. Boy, I can tell you that sure led to some big fights. Ma would be running around with all the other things to do, and sometimes when Dad and the hired man Howard came in from the barn for dinner, Ma wasn't even in the kitchen and nothing was started. Sometimes they would wait and sometimes they wouldn't because part of the deal with Howard was that he would get an evening meal. The earlier evening meal thing never really worked.

By the already-chilly days of September, when the potatoes need to be dug up, we kids are already back in school. The sun of the day and the chill of the night have, by then, dried out the lovely green of the potato plant to a withered brown, and it's time to get the potatoes into a pile in the corner of the cellar. To harvest the potatoes, Dad or my brother Sam uses a horse-drawn rake with three teeth that dig into the ground through the rows of potatoes and dig them up so they lie on top of the dirt waiting for us kids to pick them up.

To get potatoes from the fields to the house, Dad hitches a horse to a wagon that he loads with empty bushel baskets. He hands out the baskets to us in the potato patch, then comes back to pick them up when they are full. At first we got three cents a bushel for picking potatoes and now, a couple of years later, it is up to five cents a bushel. It isn't easy once the baskets are getting full to keep dragging them behind us until they are full. There is no way to get sneaky. After all, my father is the one who is going to come back to pick up the full baskets.

It is so very hard to get five dollars together, which is the amount of money needed to save the soul of a native in Africa. If we save one soul, we are sure to go straight to heaven. It sure is awfully nice to be able to count how much money I made at the end of each potato picking day. I wonder if there are more ways to be very sure that I will go straight to heaven, because sometimes it's as if the day will never come when I will have five dollars.

Several times, when things have been really bad, especially with so many kids, I heard Ma and Dad whisper about maybe some of us would have to be sent away. I don't know where we might be sent, or if I would be one of the kids sent away. That kind of talk sure makes for awful scary thinking and dreaming.

25

Starching and Ironing Clothes ~ Babysitter

I so much want our house to look nice like Mr. and Mrs. Smith's house and Aunt Cora and Uncle Ed's house, but then Mrs. Smith has only one kid, Iris, and Aunt Cora has only about half the number of kids that we do. When the curtains in our kitchen get a little bit soiled and limp, they need to be washed and starched. Starch is made from a powder mixed with water, which my mother heats to boiling on the stove and then lets cool. After cooling, the starch looks like a very thin white pudding. We use it to stiffen clothes and curtains when they are ironed. To do this, we put water in a basin with just enough of the starch to make whatever stiffness we want in the clothes or curtains. We dip dry, clean fabric into the starch and carry the items dripping wet outdoors and hang them on the clothesline next to the playhouse to dry.

After we bring the dry, stiff clothes in the house in an oval wicker basket, we lay out a towel next to where we'll be sprinkling the clothes with water. Usually that's done on the large, oval, oilcloth-covered kitchen table. Sometimes, when the oilcloth looks real bad, Dad tacks a thin piece of linoleum to the table instead of an oilcloth that hangs over the edges. For sprinkling, we use a bottle of water topped with a rubber stopper that has a metal top with little holes in it. We shake the bottle up and down to get the water to sprinkle out on the clothes. If I can't find the bottle, all I have to do is get a dish of water, dunk my hand into the water and shake it over the dress or curtain. Doing the sprinkling by hand not only takes a long time, but it's harder to do a good job.

Next, we roll up the starched dress or curtain, keeping the roll a little shorter than the width of the towel. After rolling up something like a dress, we put it on top of the towel and roll the towel just to cover it. When seven or eight rolled up items have been added to the towel, the towel is a big, bumpy, round thing. I try to make sure to sprinkle everything with just enough water to make just the right dampness for quick ironing. Sometimes, one of us kids or Ma sprinkles a little too much water and it takes forever to iron. Or, if they're not damp enough, the clothes will be pretty wrinkled.

The bottom part of our iron is a plain piece of iron that is flat on the bottom with curved edges. It has a slightly rounded point on one end, and curves around to a three-inch straight back part. It is about five inches long and two inches thick. We have three of these iron metal bottoms, which we heat on top of the wood-burning kitchen stove. There is a metal frame that attaches to the tops of the iron bottoms. It has a handle that clamps down on the hunks of metal on top of the stove. It sure doesn't seem to take very long before I have to go back to the stove to change the one I'm using for a hotter one. If the stove itself isn't very hot, like in the summertime, it takes forever to iron the starched damp clothes—especially if the sprinkler person used too much water.

Sometimes the towel-wrapped roll of sprinkled things, which is left in its spot on the back of a little table in the downstairs bathroom, is forgotten. It's the same table that we use to change the kids' diapers as well as where clean clothes are often piled up. Someone may bring dry clothes in from the clothesline and just dump them there before folding them and putting them away. If the roll stays around for a couple of days, whatever part of clothing that is next to the towel holding it together will dry out. When that happens, it's a lot of extra work for me to try and sprinkle a little water on the dry spots when I'm ironing. Having so many kids in our family sure makes it hard to take care of everything. I wonder what it would be like in our family if there weren't so many kids. I also wonder which kids wouldn't be here.

The curtains in the dining room and the parlor are store-bought lace from the fancy days when there were only a few kids. Washing and starching the curtains for those windows is a whole different thing than doing the kitchen curtains. The lace curtains are washed, rinsed, and starched, then stretched out real tight on a big rectangular wooden frame. The size of the frame can be adjusted using a wing nut and screw at each corner. There are tiny nails in each side of the frame that are about three-fourths of an inch apart. We very carefully fasten the edges of the lace curtains to the little nails. I love it so when the curtains go back up. At least for a little while they look like all the curtains in those other houses like Aunt Cora's and the Smith's house. They are so pretty—all lacy and so clean and perfect.

One day my mother and father went off with all the other kids except me and the youngest kid in the family—Bernadette. Things started out pretty well. I'm not a sissy, but the house sure seems big when there is only a baby and me.

Besides that, it's so quiet. Our house is one that usually has kids or parents hollering or screaming about one thing or another. Bernadette started to cry real loud. There I was in the kitchen with a bawling baby, and I was kind of scared. There are flimsy curtains on the windows and no curtain on the glass in the door going out to the open porch. It was nighttime. There was no bright moon or stars, and, if anyone wanted to look in, they sure could do it through the white flimsy curtains with their yellow ruffles on the edge of the pulled back top part and the straight down bottom part. There are just so darn many windows in the kitchen. There is the one facing west with the pedal Singer sewing machine under it, then two more facing north with a clock on a little shelf between them, and the fourth one next to the door looking out onto the swing on the open porch. All the windows are pretty big. They each have two rectangles side by side on the top and the same thing on the bottom, and latch in the middle. The windows open from the middle with the bottom part going up. Altogether each window is about four feet high and about two and one-half feet wide.

It was scary with all those windows and the door with the glass in the top part, and a kid I couldn't stop from crying. There isn't any other room in the house where I would feel safer than the kitchen. After all, they all have windows. Besides, there's a rocking chair in the kitchen, and I used it to rock Bernadette to try to get her to stop crying. It was hardly a time that I could go to one of the two hiding places in the house that I dream about—the mothball closet on the second floor or the attic space over the second floor.

Of course, the first thing I did was warm a bottle of milk with a nipple to give to Bernadette. I took her to the rocking chair with the bottle and thought she would get quiet with the rocking and feeding while I hummed whatever tune came into my head. She didn't stop crying for a minute and wouldn't suck on the nipple. Next, for quite a while, I tried walking back and forth, back and forth with her. Things didn't get any better. As time went on, her cries seemed to be almost screeches as I kept getting more and more scared. One thing that had always seemed to work to quiet babies was *sucette,* so that's what I tried next. I put a piece of bread on a little cloth and tied it so the shape the bread made was a little bigger than a marble, then dunked it into warm milk. Boy, that didn't work either. She just kept balling. Of course, every little while I'd check her diaper to make sure that end was okay.

Did something happen to the family that they are gone so long? Church evening services of any kind often last so very long, especially if it's a priest who goes on and on trying to make people feel sorry for all their sins. No matter how hard anybody tries, of course, everybody sins in one way or another. I so often hear my mother say that something is the work of the devil. I wonder if it's true when she says that. There are all kinds of ways for people to sin.

Of course, mortal sins are the worst. After committing a mortal sin, people have to be very careful not to end up in hell. They had better get to confession as fast as they can, because an accident could happen and they might die and go straight to hell and never even have a chance to go to purgatory and then heaven. There are smaller sins like hoping somebody who hurts me gets hurt, and I only think it for a little minute. I think that would probably be a venial sin—at least I hope so. We all should be so very careful because there sure are an awful lot of things that can keep people from going to heaven.

I wish that, even though so many people can fit into our great big car, another kid had stayed home with me. Dad is such an awful driver. The reason he is so awful is that he just can't seem to keep his eyes off the crops that other farmers have planted in their fields along the road. He makes remarks about good or bad hay, oats, or corn with an occasional *sacre bleu*, a sort of French excuse for a curse.

Whenever we go for a ride in the car, my mother gets out her rosary beads as soon as we leave the driveway and start up the dirt road. Every single chance she gets she keeps trying to push us higher toward heaven. I sure wish that sometimes we could just ride in the car and look out the window and not have anybody say anything. I can imagine how nice that would be, but I just know that it will never happen when my mother is in the car.

I just know in my heart what a good girl I am. I don't have to be praying all the time for my sins to be forgiven. For example, one time I was sleeping in the same room as one of our hired girls, and I happened to glance up and there she was. I could see her in the closet in the mirror taking off her clothes to put on her nightgown. Of course, I turned away right away.

Sometimes I have fights with Marie, but I don't start them. She probably would say the same thing—that she never starts them. Then there's Rita, who always runs to Ma with every little thing I do that she thinks Ma would get mad about—like my being friendly with somebody my mother thinks we shouldn't be friends with. Ma seems to get mad at me a lot. I'm not sure why. I try to make her like me by doing things like helping her with the younger kids when I come home for lunch from school, but nothing seems to work.

All kinds of things kept going through my head being all alone that night with a very little baby who wouldn't stop crying. Everything felt so dark. I just hoped the family would be back soon. After all where would they all go except to church?

I have never been as glad as when I saw the car headlights coming down the road. I couldn't wait to hand over the kid—and it wasn't scary anymore with all those people around.

26

School ~ Valentine's Day

There are some things that happen in our one-room school that make me ashamed and sad. One of those things happens when Valentine's Day comes around. Actually, for a long time before that day comes, I can't wait for it to be over. There are a lot of things to worry about. I knew from almost the first grade that the Patnode kids weren't going to get many valentines. I think it was because everyone knew that if a Patnode kid gave any valentines to other kids or to Miss Carpenter, they would have to be homemade.

There she is again. That darn Antoinette—and some of the other kids—ready to hand out store-bought valentines. The day before Valentine's Day, Miss Carpenter lets us use colored paper, and sometimes she even brings in a little paper lace to help us make nicer valentines, but nobody can get them to look as fancy as the store-bought ones. Besides, I could never write down any of the mushy things that are on store-bought valentines. Are the big boys like Howard and Ross going to give out any valentines to girls? I especially would love a valentine from them, but they never do anything that all the other kids would consider to be, for a boy, a sissy thing. Besides that they know if they ever did anything like that, they would never hear the end of the teasing from all the other kids.

Valentine's Day just has to come and go. Even walking the quarter-mile dirt road to school makes me sad. When I get to school, there it is—the pretty box decorated with hearts that gives out all the hurts. It is about the size of two shoe boxes together. It has a letter-size opening in the top for the valentines. There are a lot of nervous giggles, but I just know I won't be one of the kids giggling.

Kids like Antoinette always get Miss Carpenter an extra big fancy valentine. I don't know how Miss Carpenter can help but like Antoinette better than me when she does things like that and, on top of that, her mother never complains about anything. Miss Carpenter tells us about how the earth and animals were made and that it wasn't by God. Good Catholics know that everything started with Adam and Eve and the snake, so you can just imagine how much complaining my mother had to do to straighten out Miss Carpenter.

I put two or three homemade valentines into the box to people like Antoinette, because she is a girl and in the same class as me, and to Miss Carpenter. I have to be very careful because, no matter how much I might want to send a valentine to a boy, I never do that. My brothers and sisters watch real close for things like that, and their teasing isn't very nice. Even when they don't see anything special, they say mean things—like I am boy crazy. I have to be very careful not to do things like sitting next to a boy or talking to one. When Miss Carpenter calls us to the front of the room to sit on the six-foot-long bench for some school work that she is putting on the blackboard, it gets pretty hard to know what to do when I end up sitting next to a boy.

I love recess. There are three swings in the front of the schoolhouse and a set of six-inch rings on chains that are about four feet off the ground. That is one place where I can have fun and show off and probably not get teased—of course that's unless I'm wearing a dress and some kid gets a peek or two up the skirt. I love to make the swings go a little higher than the ten-foot-high bar that holds them. Way up there, the chain loosens and jerks in the sky before it starts to come down again. It is a little scary, but show-off things can be that way.

Something else I love is playing softball. I had to grow up a little before the big boys let me get in the game—certainly it wasn't before I was in fourth grade. I sure am better at hitting the ball than my sisters and the other girls. None of them even likes to play softball—well, at least not anywhere near as much as I do—and my big brother Sam. At home, if anybody tries to start a ball game before Ma gets us in the house for prayers, it is Sam or me.

Finally, it is time to get the valentines out of the box. Miss Carpenter always lets one of the bigger kids reach into that awful box and call out the names. My heart always beats so fast. I just know that there might not even be a single one for me. It takes forever, and as the last ones are coming out, I am lucky if I get a single one. I feel so bad I want to cry, but of course, I can't do that. After all, every single kid knows that only sissies cry. I wonder if any other kid gets as sad inside as I do. That sure isn't something I can talk about. Some kids have to be hurt pretty bad—like a very bad cut—before they cry. Of course, the big boys never cry no matter what.

It's hard being a farm kid from a very big Catholic family where we are encouraged to do so many things to try and not go to hell. We may never miss mass and Communion on Sundays and holy days of obligation. Then there's confession, endless morning and night prayers, stations of the cross, and pledges not to do bad things like drinking and smoking. We even know not to play with non-Catholics or even Catholics who don't do all the things that good Catholics do. There is no way that I won't play with another kid if I get a chance, especially since I think the most I would get for that is a venial sin. Most teachers, mothers, fathers, kids—just about all people—are missing at least a few points that could send them straight to heaven.

I have so many dreams. I know I am a good girl. I just know that if I were somewhere where nobody knew all the rules about sinning and church, and they just knew me, they would like me. All they did know was my not saying anything bad, like asking questions about God or whether I liked boys, or there weren't a whole lot of other kids around trying to be extra holy—just me, that little kid, they would like me. People don't seem to ever think I am a little kid because I am bigger than other girls my age. Even in the fourth grade I was already starting to get boobs. As soon as any girl starts to show boobs, my mother sure takes care of that in a hurry. The Sears and Roebuck catalog has brassieres that are made like two tied-together saucers in front that sure keep me pretty flat. That is probably just as well, because the boys start to make nasty jokes as soon as a girl has even little bumps.

The seats and desks in our school are fastened together. They are lined up next to the windows on the south side of the room and face west toward the teacher's desk. The walls on the west and north side are solid walls. On the west wall, and a little to the right of the teacher's desk, is a roll-down, five-by-four-foot map of the world. In front of the map is the teacher's big wooden desk with her chair in back of it facing us kids. On her left, about five feet from her desk and ten feet away from a blackboard, is a six-foot wooden bench for us to sit on when Miss Carpenter is using the blackboard for lessons.

The blackboard takes up the space between the world map and the northwest corner of the room and continues on the north wall for another eight feet. Whenever a kid wants to make a little trouble, all of a sudden there is that awful, scratchy sound of a fingernail being pulled over the blackboard. There is a small wooden tray about three inches wide running along the base of the blackboard. That is where white chalk, a few colored chalks, and black, one-by-five inch, two inch thick felt blackboard erasers are kept.

I don't think there is one single kid who doesn't try to be the kid Miss Carpenter asks to take the blackboard erasers outside to smack against each other to get the chalk dust beat out of them. It is so much fun when Miss Carpenter takes out a new box of chalk. At last, to be using a long chalk instead of the mostly little pieces, which are all that are left by the time she opens a new box. Usually, the new chalk is white but, around Christmas or Easter, she sometimes brings out a box of colored chalk.

At Christmastime, we have a Christmas tree in the southwest corner of the room, which is to the right of Miss Carpenter. Miss Carpenter sometimes has us do little plays to which our mothers and fathers are invited. Dad doesn't come, but sometimes Ma does. We string a wire across the room from the south wall, in front of Miss Carpenter's desk, all the way to the blackboard on the north wall. Over the wire we pin some white sheets. I love being in a play where I can be good at playing somebody else, and then be told I did a good job. The curtain on one side is left closed, and that's where we change into whatever we need to for our part in the play. Of course, the other side is pushed back whenever we are ready to start the play. I think I am probably one of the best ones in plays, but then that's probably the same thing that other kids think about themselves.

The only windows in our one-room schoolhouse are on the south wall and run almost the whole length of the wall. During winter, between the kettle of water on the potbellied stove, us kids, and the teacher, there is enough moisture in the air that beautiful, delicate, lacy-looking frost covers the windows. What a wonderful magic way to dream—looking at the frost. It's so different from all the rough stuff with brothers and sisters and the hard work on the farm or moms and dads fighting—it is just so beautiful. Then when I reach over and touch the frosty dream, it just melts away. It sure doesn't seem to take very long before Miss Carpenter catches me dreaming and tells me to get back to my schoolwork.

For special times like Thanksgiving and Christmas, we hang designs on the windows that we have cut from heavy colored paper. It is such fun, even if we have a hard time getting them to stay up. We make paper Christmas trees or animals for Christmas, turkeys for Thanksgiving, and colorful flowers in springtime. There is a little wall space between two windows that has a picture of a farm family standing together in a hayfield. The man is holding a three-prong pitchfork. They all look very sad and hardworking.

Over the coat hooks in back of the room is a bulletin board. That is the place where we might find our names on an honor list if we do something special like get a gold star for a spelling or a math test—or even a silver star. Sometimes it's a picture we colored that is put up there for everybody to see. It sure makes me feel proud when I get something special tacked up, whether it's a pretty picture or that I get a good enough grade to be on the bulletin board—especially since we almost never get any praise at home. Springtime is when Miss Carpenter makes pictures for us to color. I am very careful to make the colors soft and very pretty.

It means so much to me to have my pictures on the bulletin board. My sisters don't seem to care.

27

Christmas at Our House ~ A Porcupine

Sometimes I think of Christmas as one of the best times of the year and other times one of the worst. Probably Ma and Dad can't think about Christmas the way that we kids or some other people think about Christmas because, when we were little kids up to about six years old, we believed in Santa Claus. When I was a very little kid, like my younger brothers and sisters, I would ask my oldest sister Rita what the secret was that she and the next-to-the-oldest sister Marie were whispering about. She made me so mad—she would always say, "You'll find out in your later years." I wasn't big enough to hit her.

The first thing we do to start getting ready for Christmas is to get a spruce tree out of the forest for our Christmas tree. There are almost no evergreens on our farm that would make good Christmas trees. The few scraggily ones are way up the little mountain in back of the barn then west somewhere in the woods of the day pasture. Even if we could find a tree, there probably wouldn't be much left of the branches by the time we dragged it all the way down the mountain and back to the house.

We go into our neighbor Mr. George Smith's north pasture, which is in back of his barn, or in the Trombley pasture just west of our house to get a tree. It's even hard to find a good tree in their pastures. I always feel a little funny about getting a tree off their land without asking permission. After all, if they see us, Dad or Sam will be carrying an ax, and, if we've already cut the tree, they'll see it trailing behind us in the snow. I worry about what they might say if they see us.

Sometimes when we're looking for a tree, ice and snow cover a little stream that we don't know about. After all, we are in George Smith's night pastureland or the Trombley day pasture, and none of us is familiar with where a little running stream might be hiding. One time, down I went with a kind of crunchy sound through the first layer of snow, then through the ice into the water. I was wearing rubber boots. The water came over the top of one of my boots. Boy, I sure was awfully cold. The others were near a good spruce to cut down, so there was no way that anybody was going to go home with me and without the tree. The trip home sure seemed like a long way with one slushy boot.

It seems such a shame to cut down a Christmas tree. It isn't going to live very long, and it smells so good and looks so pretty. It is sort of like killing a deer or something like that and dragging it through the snow back to the house. I think maybe I wouldn't feel so bad if there were more spruce and pine trees in the forest.

I like trees a lot. There are all the wonderful maples in the sugar bush that give out their sap in the spring for maple syrup. Then there are the much littler trees in the mysterious forest where the trees are only about fifteen feet high and so close together that the sun barely comes through the leaves in the summertime.

Cows usually don't go into the mysterious forest because there is almost no grass. The leaves from the trees keep most of the sunshine out. No matter how hot it gets, by the end of August it's always cool in that forest. The ground is covered in leaves that have fallen over the years, and all that is left is a damp, rich soil covering. There is a scent that is not quite musty—just a nice earthy smell.

One time I was walking while leading Kit through the mysterious forest. The middle-sized, reddish brown dog who goes after the cows with me followed us into the forest. I was only about one hundred feet into the forest when, out of the corner of my eye, I saw a quick movement. The movement stopped. I looked more closely. My goodness, it was a porcupine. I had never seen one before, but I had heard about them. It rolled into a ball with only its long quills sticking out all over its body.

The dog started moving toward the porcupine. I screamed for it to stop, but it just kept going. It was all just too awful. The dog grabbed the porcupine and started to violently shake it back and forth as I continued to scream. Finally he let it go. What an awful sight. Quills were sticking out of his nose and mouth, and some were even sticking out of his back. He was pawing frantically at himself. I mounted the horse and, crying hysterically, started for home as fast as I could. Halfway down the mountain, I was screaming hoping my father would come running as soon as we got back to the barn. My father cut the ends off the quills then pulled them out with pliers. I couldn't watch. The poor dog had to know my father was trying to help because all he did during this awful puling out of the quills was to whimper loudly. Later on, I saw the body of the dead porcupine in the forest. My father, as well as other farmers, said they had never heard of a dog actually killing a porcupine.

Back to Christmastime. After Dad fits the spruce tree into a tree holder, he stands it up in the corner of the dining room in front of the door to the porch. Now Ma and we kids get to do the rest of the Christmas decorating. The tree looks really nice if Ma or Dad buys some tinsel. When that happens, there is only one small box. Every single piece is put on the tree very carefully. Next we add a few bright-colored bulbs, and, for the very top of the tree, a Christmas angel from years past. All we kids string popcorn on twine and hang it on the tree. Some of the other things that come out every year from the mothball closet are one-inch-thick red and green paper strands that form a paper rope. Some pieces are hung on the tree. The rest is crisscrossed to each corner of the ceiling and held up where they cross in the middle by a big red paper bell hung on the light fixture over the dining room table.

One of the very best things about Christmas is when there is a ten-pound bucket of candy that is divided into three parts. One part has ribbon candy, one popcorn, and one chocolates with cream centers. Sometimes, in a year when we have been especially poor, there isn't a bucket of candy and there aren't any presents for the bigger kids. If, during the year, there hasn't been enough rain or snow, or there is too much rain or snow, and extra hay or grain has to be bought on credit from the GLF store, there sure isn't going to be money used for presents for the big kids in the family. Another thing that makes a big difference is the money that Sealtest pays for farmers' milk. Of course, mothers and fathers never talk to kids about stuff like that. Mostly we learn about it by how unhappy people are with each other. I don't think that's the way it should be, but there sure isn't anything kids can do about things like that.

I know that, if I were awfully good, most of the time what I should be thinking about most at Christmas is about baby Jesus being born. After all, that's why there is a Christmas. But I sure wish I didn't have to worry about not getting anything at all. When the kids in my family are going to start school, and sometimes even if they are already past the first grade, we might get a pencil box. That is such a wonderful present.

One year my brother Sam got an Erector Set. Boy, is it fancy. It came in a flat, red, metal box about two feet by one and one-half feet and five inches deep. The set came with an electric motor and a whole lot of all kinds of metal pieces to build different things with. He keeps the set on the floor next to his bed. I sure know better than to play with the Erector Set. I'm sure it would be one more time he would be mean to me.

My mother is always trying to encourage us to be nuns, so, if any girl gets a doll, it will be a nun doll. Nun dolls always look the same, with a white head cover, a long black dress, white long underwear and socks, and black shoes. I sure would like a fancy doll with a beautiful bonnet, lots of curls, and a fancy dress, but a nun doll is sure a lot better than not getting one at all.

Sometimes for Christmas there are family games that any kid can play with. Some of the games are Chinese checkers, pick-up-sticks, dominos, puzzles, and Lincoln Logs. I wish there was more time to play, even though there always seem to be parts missing or very few parts left from any one of the games when there is a chance to play with them.

Midnight mass starts at the end of Christmas Eve and is the beginning of Christmas day. The mass is so very special. Just before the mass, I like to go and kneel before the big manger in front of Saint Joseph's statue. The manger is about four feet by two feet and two and a half feet high. The baby Jesus is lying down in a little bed of straw with his mother Mary kneeling over him looking at him with adoring eyes while Joseph stands close by.

Baby Jesus looks as if he is too fragile to have been a living baby. His skin is the color of faint pink and white porcelain that looks as if he might bruise if he were touched. He looks so fragile and so beautiful. In back of those three figures are the animals, then, outside the manger, stand the three wise men with their gifts for baby Jesus. When I'm in church, with the smell of incense, the flickering candles, and the nativity scene, it sure is easy, for at least a little while, not to think about what I might be getting or not getting for Christmas.

Back home, the younger kids who believe in Santa Claus are very happy to leave a snack out for him. They think he might leave more things for them. That is one thing that is nice about being a younger kid—you believe in Santa and are sure you will get something for Christmas. Dad isn't involved in anything about Christmas except cutting down the tree and putting it in a stand and going to mass. Ma and Dad don't seem any happier around Christmastime than at other times of the year. I don't know why.

28

Grandma ~ Cats

I expect my Grandma Langevin is a lot like most grandmas. She never hugs or kisses people except for a few very special ones. She sure doesn't hug or kiss any of us Patnode kids. She gives a very little kiss to my four nun aunts when she sees them. They are her very own children, and everybody knows how proud she is of them. Their pictures and that of her youngest son Uncle Joe in his sailor uniform are on top of her dressers and tables. Sometimes she is in a picture with the nuns, and sometimes it is just the four of them. There aren't many smiles in the nun pictures. In Uncle Joe's pictures, there he is with that great big smile on his handsome face. I'm sure I would love him, but I've only seen him once or twice. It is no wonder my grandmother likes him the best of her four sons. Of course, she would have liked him even more if he had been a priest. Maybe some day I'll have a boyfriend who looks like my Uncle Joe.

In the pictures, the nuns are almost always in their habits—long black dresses down to the floor with black laced shoes sometimes peeping out from under the habits. Usually, their hands are tucked under what looks a little like a long black apron over the black dress. They wear a wide, round white collar and their heads, foreheads, ears, and necks are covered by a tight-fitting white cloth. Over this cloth on their heads is a black veil that falls down to a little past their shoulders. My sisters and I often play at being nuns with black make-believe dresses and white diapers over our heads that are tied under our chins. Ma never stops us when we are playing at being nuns.

Ma sure lets us know how much she wants us to be nuns. I wonder if she would like me more if I talked about being a nun. She sure seems to like Rose a lot more than she likes me. Could it be because Rose is so pretty and never ever talks back? Besides that, Rose has the same black hair and brown eyes as my mother. My father has gray hair, but I think that before the gray it was the same color as mine—brown. And we both have blue eyes. Could it be that's why Dad seems to like me the best? At least that's what I think. Or is it because I am the girl who helps out the most of all the girls doing barn chores and other things like raking the hay in the summer? I wonder if other kids think about things like that.

Back to Grandma. She has lived in two different houses in Ellenburg Corners besides the one she lives in now. There is a little river about twenty feet across that runs through Ellenburg Corners. There are a lot of rocks in the river that stick out so the water tumbles over them with gurgles and gentle splashes. The moving water sure looks pretty, and sometimes I can see a few little speckled trout darting here and there. I would love to go down and play in the river bed, but I'm sure one of my brothers or sisters would tell Grandma or Ma and they would get real mad at me. In the spring, with all the snow melting, the water gets to as much as three feet deep. It looks so powerful. I think that, if somebody fell in, they wouldn't get out alive from being bashed into the rocks as they flew down the river. By July and August, it's always back down to its gentle, rather slow-moving, one foot deep. The river goes right through the middle of Ellenburg Corners and on toward Ellenburg Depot.

The first house my grandmother lived in is on the west side of the river next to a store on the edge of the river. There is a scary, very old bridge over the river next to the store. It was closed off and abandoned for a new bridge a very long time ago. In fact, I can't remember it ever being used by cars or horses and wagons. The new bridge was built a couple hundred feet away from the old bridge. The old bridge is held up by the most rusted iron I've ever seen. The part that goes over the river is made of wooden planks on top of the rusted iron beams. There are many places where the planks are missing, and the ones that remain are so dry and shrunken they look as if they wouldn't be able to hold even a kid's weight. But, of course, only sissies don't walk across the old bridge.

The second house Grandma lived in is on the north side of the Patnode road. It is just a couple of houses from the main road and the newer bridge. There is a family of Patnodes that lives farther down the road who aren't related to us. A man from that family is one of the teachers in the big school. Whenever anybody says anything about them, my mother and father stick up their noses as if they don't like them. I don't think those Patnodes go to church, so no wonder my parents act the way they do. I still would like to meet them to decide for myself if they are nice people. Of course, there is no way for that to happen.

I remember that second house best because of my grandmother's wonderful orange cat. My grandmother and my mother don't like cats. In fact, they act as if they hate cats, but this cat is very special. Some cats are kept around to get rid of mice. This cat is a wonderful mouser. She sometimes brings a mouse to where we can see her with it. Maybe she is bragging. Sometimes she even catches rats. One time, we were having an awful problem with rats at our house in Ellenburg, so Ma borrowed Grandmas' orange cat. What can anybody expect from one poor cat? She couldn't help with that much of a problem. Boy, I can tell you that was one time when there were a lot of extra prayers flying up to heaven to try and get rid of the rats. (I don't know why, but heaven is always "up there" and hell is always "down there.") The cat went back to Grandma's. Ma doesn't let us have cats in our house. I feel real bad that she won't let me have a cat in the house. Any cats around have to either stay down in the cellar or outdoors or in the barn.

At Grandma's house she had the same kind of chamber pots under the beds as Aunt Cora has under hers. The pots with no covers were for number one and the ones with covers were for number two. I didn't use the pot at her second house because there are certain things you just don't do around Grandma—or try very hard not to do. I always go to the outhouse out back just before I go to bed. The chamber pots make noise when we use them, especially when we are piddling. At Aunt Cora's we try to do the same thing—go to the outhouse just before we go to bed. Both Grandma's and Aunt Cora's outhouses are attached to the outside of the woodshed and, like all outhouses, they are not heated. It is so hard to potty in an outhouse in the winter when it is so bitter cold, with the north wind blowing in between the cracks in the twelve-inch-wide boards that make up the walls. It sure is awful cold on bare bottoms. The potty places to sit down are just two holes cut out of a wooden board. I'm not sure why there are two holes. I can't imagine two people pottying in an outhouse at the same time.

The house that Grandma lives in now is over a store. There are two people who, at one time, lived with Grandma in the house. One was Grandpa Langevin, who was a nice, cheerful sort of old man. He smoked a pipe that Grandma didn't like. Now grumpy Uncle Ed lives there with her. I don't know if Grandma owned or paid rent in the first two houses, or in the one that they live in now. The fact that this third house is over a store sure makes things interesting. When she sends us to the store for something, instead of going down the front steps to outside, then in the front door of the store, we go the back way through her house. The path starts in her kitchen then goes down a narrow hall that has a bathroom to the left and the bedroom wall on the right, and on to Grandma's very large work/storage room, then down a flight of stairs through the storage room of the store, and on to the store.

The people who own the store keep all kinds of things in their back room. Boy, I can tell you that if there ever was a good chance to steal and probably get away with it would be to take something out of that room. There is no way that I can help myself from thinking about how easy it would be to steal when I look at candy and cookies that we almost never have at home. But there is the whole thing about heaven and hell that makes me not steal. Imagine if I stole something and then I died before I had a chance to go to confession or to tell God how sorry I was, or couldn't make God really believe I was sorry. Would I go to hell? Hell sure keeps kids from doing bad thing—if they think about things like that.

I sure like Grandma's cooking. Whenever I stay at her house, dinner is always the same. There is just one helping of each thing for grandchildren visitors. Dinner is one small potato, a small piece of meat—or fish on Friday—one other vegetable, and a slice of bread with margarine. Sometimes there is a cookie or a piece of cake for dessert. Of course, it's better than eating at my house where things are so often up in the air from the meal not being ready. Then there is usually a fight over who will wash the dishes. At Grandma's there aren't second helpings, but the food she cooks is so good and done just right. I know not to ask for second helpings because Grandma cooks just enough for one helping of each thing for everybody except for Uncle Ed. He is the uncle who has had about thirty operations since he was almost killed in the Lyon Mountain coal mine a lot of years ago.

The rocking chair in the corner of Grandma's kitchen is where Grandpa Langevin sat smoking his pipe when he was alive. Now it's where Uncle Ed sits. Grandpa is buried in the fancy cemetery on the south side of the road between Ellenburg Corner and Ellenburg Depot. The cemetery is set back about three hundred feet from the road. There are mourning stone figures of angels on each side of the entrance. About two hundred feet in back of the angels is a circle two hundred feet across with ten-foot-tall evergreens around the edge of circle. The evergreens are so thick that I can't see through them from the road. Inside the circle is a tombstone where my grandfather Langevin is buried. On the tombstone are his name and the name of my grandmother, because we all know that is where my grandmother is supposed to be buried next to her husband when she dies. Of course, the date of her death will be added after she is buried there.

It seems as if Grandma only talks to us to tell us to do something or not to do something or when she is bragging about our wonderful Buffalo cousins or her nun "children" or one of her "boys." If Grandma ever bragged about me or praised me for anything—even once—I just know I would remember every word for the rest of my life.

My other grandparents, whose names are down on their tombstones as Patenaude, are buried in the old cemetery in back of St. Edmund's Church in Ellenburg Corners. I wish I could have met them. Nobody ever talks about them. I think that is probably what most other farmer families do—not talk very much, or probably not at all, about things like dead people or feeling sad, or even feeling happy about something. People sure talk about things when they are mad, though. Most people don't seem very happy to me.

So, after Grandpa died, the chair in the corner of the kitchen became Uncle Ed's. It is very hard for him to move around. He uses what looks like a metal rod with a strap handle to support himself as he lurches forward with every step. He never looks at us with his haunted eyes, which peer out of his angry, drawn face. He almost never says anything—even to Grandma.

One of the more awful things that happens on a farm is what farmers do with kittens. My brother Sam is usually the one to do this. If there are three or four big cats already around the barn, when a new batch of kittens from one of the stray cats is born, they are put into a burlap bag and drowned. We have tried pleading and hiding them, but nothing works to keep them from being killed. When people move kittens to a different place, mother cats, if they can, bring them back to where they were born. They carry them in their teeth by the back of their little baby necks.

One time one of our cats had her babies in the middle of winter. They were in the cellar of our house, where even the furnace going full blast can't keep the icy north winds from blowing through the edges of the two tiny north windows. There is a very small potbellied woodstove with tiny legs that sits on a little table in a corner of the bathroom on the first floor. The stove helps to warm the bathroom. I found a cardboard box that would fit under the table. When nobody was looking, I went down into the cellar and brought up the little babies to the bed I made for them in the box under the stove. Of course, I couldn't keep them from crying when their mother wasn't around. My mother heard them. She threw them and the mother down the cellar steps.

Sometimes a farm is a cruel place.

29

School Picnics ~ Grandma

Grandpa Langevin was the one person out of all of my relatives—aunts, uncles, sisters, and brothers—who kind of laughed over not much of anything. He was a nice old man who smoked a pipe as he sat in his rocking chair in the corner of the kitchen. He would smile at us and talk to us—I can't remember about what. I even liked the smell of his smoking pipe. I must have been pretty little when he died because the next person to sit in that same corner is my grumpy old limping Uncle Ed. He sits there and never looks in our direction. I sure wish Grandpa Langevin had lived longer. Maybe he would have helped me put puzzles together that Grandma had, or other friendly things like that.

Uncle Ed had a very bad accident at the mining company in Lyon Mountain where he worked. After the accident, he was operated on about thirty times. I guess I might have been grumpy and sad-looking all the time if that had happened to me. There is one time each year when I keep hoping that maybe he might change just a little bit. The mining company pays for him to go to Florida for a three- or four-week vacation every winter. When he comes back, he always brings a bag of oranges for our family.

Those oranges are the only ones we get all year, which makes it particularly wonderful to get them. Because he buys the oranges, I feel good toward him and look a little bit more in his direction hoping he will say something or maybe even look friendly, but he never does no matter how many times I stay overnight at Grandma's. Grandma takes very good care of Uncle Ed. She always feeds him his meals before she feeds us. I like the way Grandma cooks. She's careful, and everything is always "just so." She puts a piece of meat, a potato, and one other vegetable on his plate. He can ask for more, but usually he doesn't.

I don't know how Uncle Ed manages to fish and bring back eels. They are snakelike fish that Grandma cooks when he brings them home. When I see them jumping around in the frying pan, even though they have already been cut into three or four pieces, the first thing I think about is snakes. The idea of eating something like a snake seems awful. They do smell good by the time they come to the table, and I'm always hungry so, of course, with Grandma giving us only one small helping of everything, down it goes—and actually the eels even taste quite good.

One of the things that Grandma bakes that tastes better than anything else in the whole world is Toll House cookies. She makes them with butter, an egg, brown and white sugar, flour, vanilla extract, and then she adds the most wonderful part—chocolate chips. Sometimes she even puts in walnuts.

Sometimes Grandma goes to her daily mass, and I don't go with her. If the cookie jar is about two-thirds full, that is the best time to snitch a couple of cookies. I take out the cookies and move a few around hoping she will not be able to tell. I wonder if she does know and just doesn't say anything. It's funny thinking about things like that. Snitching these cookies is sort of like snitching our neighbor Mrs. Smith's doughnuts. Is snitching cookies and doughnuts a sin? There sure isn't anybody I can ask; and I want the cookies and doughnuts so badly that I take the chance.

Grandma never smiles, but a nice thing is that she never yells as she moves around very fast doing things. In fact, she never gets mad at me like my mother does. I am a good kid even if my mother quite often doesn't seem to think so. I so very much want my mother to like me, but she probably can't be really happy being pregnant all the time and taking care of so many kids, and then worrying about hell because of all the ways everybody commits sins.

I think life is probably hard for anybody who thinks a lot about all the things that are sins and who is careful all the time to be in a state of grace. Maybe there aren't many happy people anywhere. At least all the people trying to make sure they are going to go to heaven might find it hard to be happy. I wonder how many people that is. Grandpa never seemed to want to be doing things like saying the rosary, praying, and going to church all the time and he seemed quite happy. I wonder.

Between Ellenburg Depot and Ellenburg Corners, next to the little river that goes by Grandma's house and runs through the three Ellenburgs, is a very wonderful place for a picnic. Once a year in the spring, a yellow school bus takes the kids from our one-room schoolhouse to this special place where some of the kids go swimming. Miss Carpenter gets together a lot of picnic things to take with us. Going on the picnic is so exciting, except that I don't know how to swim, and there we all are at a place that is deep enough. Oh well, that sure wouldn't be a place to try and learn with all the other kids around to make fun of me—even if I had a bathing suit. From our schoolhouse, the bus goes down the one-mile, bumpy dirt road, heading north to the black tar road. Then we travel three miles east to Ellenburg Corner. From there the road goes a few feet north over the bridge then east down a tar road that follows the river on the right for a couple of miles toward Ellenburg Depot. At last we turn right onto a narrow dirt road with large rocks peeping through the dirt, then over a small rickety bridge over the river. A few hundred feet more, then we make a right turn where there is the most wonderful place for a picnic.

The spot is in a clearing in the middle of a forest and next to the river, which splashes over big and little rocks. The woodsy smell of the earth, trees, and grass rises to greet us. Everything is so much like, and still so different from, my treasured woods back at the family farm. What is missing on our farm—which I would like to have so very much—is the splashing sparkling beautiful water, which is deep enough for learning how to swim. Even though I don't have a swimsuit except my hidden blue one, the school picnic is always such an adventure.

Even though our little Ellenburg Center farm brook is very small and can't compare to our school picnic area with its forty-foot-wide river, I love it too. The little stream on our farm is big enough to provide water for the cows when they are in the pasture. It's about six feet across and it, too, sparkles when the sun splashes against the small rocks and pebbles. Sometimes we kids try to catch its little speckled fish with a stick we rigged up with a hanging piece of twine with a worm on a bent hook at the end. The stream never seems angry—not even when snow is melting and it gets quite deep. Sometimes in the spring, with the stream is full of melting snow, water goes over the edge past its usual boundary. We might get wet feet when we try to get across, but nobody will die from drowning. The water isn't deep enough.

At the school picnic area, when we go in the late spring, the river is rushing to somewhere else from all the snow and ice that has melted in the last couple of months. The rocks in the river look huge as the water hits them so hard that it throws up a white spray. The riverbank and picnic area are so very pretty, with big maple trees and some evergreens. In the forest, among the trees and the many moss-covered rocks, are a few wild flowers and thin grass. There are a few wooden picnic tables with attached boards for sitting.

The big boys soon disappear. Several hundred feet down the river to the east, I can see deeper water with no rocks sticking out, then the edge of a waterfall. A little past the base of the waterfall is where the big boys go to swim. We can't see them, but all the kids talk about it. The waterfall is pretty darn scary. The water is all calm just before it hits the edge of the waterfall, then it makes an angry splash against the dam that holds it back, and then it splashes down, making a muffled roar when it hits the bottom.

Miss Carpenter always brings good things to the picnic that we never have at home. The two best are hot dogs with mustard and ketchup, and store-bought cakes and cookies. Of course, potato chips and hot dog buns are pretty wonderful too. A couple of years ago—I'm a little ashamed to say—I ate twelve hot dogs! At first I ate them with buns and everything, but it kept getting harder and harder to get one by mixing in with all the other kids who were going back to the table for the hot dogs. In the end, I sort of moved past the table and took them when no one seemed to be looking. I don't know how I ever managed to get up to twelve, or why I didn't get sick, but it sure was wonderful to be able to eat that many just once.

I'm not sure how I can feel so alone most of the time and be in the middle of so many people. Talking to God sometimes helps. He feels close when I'm in church because there he is in a chalice in back of the door of his little house on the altar. At mass, the chalice comes out of the little house. During the mass the little white round flat breads that are God are put on our tongues by the priest. Of course that is only after we make our First Holy Communion. To get ready for that most holy day of our lives, we have to know a lot of stuff. We learn from a catechism—a little book that tells us all about God and sin, and how to go to confession so we can be all cleaned up from our sins before we are going to have God put on our tongues. How awful it would be to not be all white, and still black from sin, then have him put right there on our tongues. I wonder how bad he would punish us for that.

It is very hard when I go to confession on Saturday night and then I try to not have one bad thought or commit any other sin before Sunday morning mass. Confession always starts when I say, "Forgive me, Father, for I have sinned." Then I say how long it has been since my last confession. After that, it isn't hard to come up with a sin. I just go over the Ten Commandments of God. There is always a commandment that fits somebody doing sinful things. Even after learning the commandments and confessing any bad thoughts, like the time I wanted my oldest brother to die when he had just hit me, I never really feel like a bad girl because I know that I try hard to be a good girl and that is what God really wants. Sometimes, when I am called a bad girl, I get mixed-up feelings and I feel really awful.

Maybe I should try even harder, but I don't know how.

30

Grandma ~ Church ~ Hell

Sleeping at Grandma's house, which is over a store, is pretty good. She doesn't talk much—except to say what to do and not to do. The meals, even though we know not to ask for seconds, are sure something to look forward to. It seems as if we just keep looking at Grandma to see when she will stop praying or cleaning and head to the kitchen, where there is a stove on the north wall of the area that extends into a hall. Next is the door to the bathroom, and at the end of the hall is the door to a big storage area. In the middle of the little kitchen is a chrome-legged table with matching chairs.

If you stand in the hall entrance to Grandma's kitchen and look to the left, first is the door to Grandma's room, then a window on the west side. Next, on the north wall, is a door to the pantry and the door that leads to the dining-living room. Grumpy Uncle Ed's easy chair is in the corner, with the door to his room on his left. I sure like the pantry with its shelves of things like matching canisters of flour and sugar. The flour and sugar come from a store in a bag, then Grandma puts them in the cans. Here is also where she keeps baking soda, baking powder, vanilla extract, dishes, pots and pans, and all kinds of nice things—but, of course, the very best is Grandma's Toll House cookies.

Usually, two kids stay at Grandma's at the same time. Even though Grandma has another bedroom, the two kids sleep with Grandma in her bed. I expect that's because Grandma doesn't want to spend money on turning up the heat on the other side of her house where the other little bedroom is in winter, or maybe it's because she wants to keep track of what we're doing, or she doesn't want to have to wash another set of sheets. Grandma sleeps on the side of the bed closest to the door, with us taking up the middle and the far side spots.

I always try to get the place on the outside with the other kid in the middle. The bad part about the outside spot is that, in winter, Grandma turns on her large kerosene-burning stove to its very lowest setting, which makes it even colder for the kid on the outside. There sure isn't much heat that comes from where the

184

stove is in the middle of the living room all the way to Grandma's room. The heat has to travel from the living room, through an archway into the dining room, then through the kitchen door and on to Grandma's bedroom on the other side of the kitchen. That's why Grandma's bedroom is always freezing in winter.

Grandma snores really loud. The kid in the middle is almost always kind of wiggly, so trying to stay covered while not pulling the quilt off Grandma is very hard to do. Between Grandma's snores and trying to stay covered, it takes a long time for me to go to sleep. Sometimes when Grandma's snoring has pretty much stopped and I'm still covered with the quilt, the ticking of the alarm clocks keeps me awake as much as Grandma's snoring did. It has a face I can see in the dark, and is the only thing that gives off any light in the bedroom. It is round and about five inches across. When Grandma stops snoring, all I can hear is the darn ticktock, ticktock. I don't dare ask Grandma if she would put it in another room. Besides, maybe she needs it to get herself up in the morning for her daily trip to St. Edmund's Church for mass.

Grandma sure has a lot of holy things around her house. There are crucifixes of Jesus dying on the cross, a bigger one of Jesus hanging on a cross made of wood, pictures of things like God with his heart on the outside of his body, and the Virgin Mother holding the infant Jesus. Then, of course, there are always pictures of her four nun girls and her handsome sailor son Joe. Boy, I sure hope that, when I grow up, I have a boyfriend who looks like him.

At Grandma's there never are any pictures of us kids or of my mother and father. The only picture she has that includes my mother is the Langevin family picture of Grandma and Grandpa and all eleven of their kids before the four girls went off to St. Mary's to be nuns. I'm not sure why, but I don't think that my dad and my grandmother like each other. My mother is always trying to make my grandmother like her more. My grandmother sure doesn't talk very much, and, when she does, she never says things about us or my mom or dad like the kind of bragging things she says about the Buffalo bunch or the aunts in the convent, or Uncle Paul, or Uncle Joe. One of her children she never brags about is Uncle Rod. I wonder if that has to do with his being a farmer.

I can't figure out a way to make Grandma like me more. I'm pretty sure she thinks I'm okay, but that's all. Actually, I don't think there is any way. She doesn't talk very much when there are only people from the Patnode bunch around. I never see her hug or kiss anybody but the nuns, or ever say I love you. She talks a lot more when the nuns or the Buffalo people come to visit. They don't visit very often.

When Grandma gets to her pew in church, she genuflects and kneels in the aisle before going into her pew. Her pew is on the opposite side of the church from ours. She always kneels with her back very straight on the hard wooden kneeler she pulls down. We all like kneeling with our behinds resting on the church pew. All Grandma has to do is the same that Ma does—give us a dirty look—and we get off our behinds and kneel up straight.

Even though I very much want Grandma to like me, it is not enough to make me go to church with her every day when school is out. After all, when I'm home, there are a lot of prayers every morning and even more every night, and mass on Sunday, with very long sermons. There is so darn much about sinning in sermons—then more of the same from my mother at home. Sin here. Sin there. Sin everywhere. I wonder if people like the nuns sin very much. What kind of sins do they confess? Do they have bad thoughts like wanting to hit somebody, or, maybe if someone is being awfully mean to them, maybe even wishing they were dead?

I sure wish that I didn't have to worry so much about sin. I feel like such a good girl, but how can I be a really good girl when there is so much in the sermons, the prayers to God, and the catechism about sin? Is almost everybody in a state of venial or mortal sin all the time? I wonder what my brothers and sisters and my mom and dad say when they go to confession. Do they worry a lot about which place they will go to after they die—purgatory or heaven or hell?

Maybe that's why I so much like going after the cows in the pasture on horseback and raking the hay. Because, when I'm doing things like that, I can't be doing a sin and I can be thinking nice things. I have mostly good thoughts when I look at the blue of the sky with its floating puffy white clouds, the shape of the green leaves on trees, the gray of the rocks, the yellow of the flowers, the green tufts of grass—even when I smell the lovely earthy smells. There is comfort in looking at wild birds, other little animals, and water gently murmuring over little protruding rocks.

I wish I could talk to somebody. It would be so nice to be able to talk about church, school, boys, and all kinds of things. Actually, there isn't one brother or sister who, if I told them some of the secret things that I feel in my heart, I could trust not to say anything to somebody else.

I wonder if heaven is as wonderful as kids are told, and if purgatory is sort of okay because after a while we will go to heaven. Of course, how long a soul stays in purgatory depends on how many venial sins are left on a person's soul when he or she dies. Hell has got to be awful—burning and knowing it will never stop. I wonder if hell is worse for the souls of people who have a lot of mortal sins when they die. I sure am trying hard to never ever be out of a state of grace when I die. Hell just sounds so terrible. I've seen pictures of the fires of burning hell, with the horned devil standing in the middle of all the bad people holding his fork, where they are going to be forever. It must be even worse than anybody can imagine.

31

Winter ~ Snow ~ A Bar

The dirt road next to our house runs north for one mile, then it meets the main tar road that runs east and west. To the west is Ellenburg Center with its two stores. The main store is the one owned by my Uncle Bill and another man. The other store has fancy kinds of sewing things. The lady who owns it doesn't sell food or candy, so my uncle's store is the important one for farm and village people.

There is a place in the village that my mother and father think is evil—a bar. I know about that bar from hearing my parents talk so much about things being either good or bad. It seems so hard to be good and so easy to be bad. Beer is sold at the bar in Ellenburg Center, and I'm pretty sure other bad things go on. We know about the family that owns the bar and live upstairs over it. My mother and father do a lot of whispering whenever they think that is where my brother Sam goes when he disappears. After all, if he visits the family on the second floor, he might very well visit the bar on the first floor.

My family's first kid is my brother Sam. He is named after my father, Sam. After that came three girls then me, which means that Sam is considered to be very important in my family. Everybody on a farm knows how important boys' and men's muscles are for the many heavy chores. Their strength is needed for all kinds of things like moving heavy bags of oats and large forkfuls of hay, hitching up teams of horses, and driving them. It seems that no matter what Sam does, there isn't much said to him but, when he disappears, we hear the whispers.

What makes any drinking that Sam might do really bad is that he took the pledge in church, along with the rest of us, to never drink anything that has alcohol in it. As if that isn't bad enough, he made friends with the bar owner's family. I heard in the whispers that sometimes he even visits upstairs where there is at least one girl in the family. That is especially bad considering how careful my mother and father are about things that might lead to lord knows what—maybe his even marrying into a family that owns a bar where, of course, he would be around drinking people all the time. What temptations that would bring him.

Next to Uncle Bill's store in Ellenburg Center is a long shed about forty feet by twelve feet. The side that faces west has no wall. The single-panel roof is about ten feet high in back and slants to seven feet in front. There are walls on both ends and the back of the shed. This is where farmers who come to Uncle Bill's store, or some other place nearby, leave their horses. Sometimes, if the horses have been fighting big snowbanks on unplowed roads and cutting across fields or galloping, by the time they get to Uncle Bill's store and are put in the shed, steam is coming up from their bodies. Of course, if it is bitter cold, there is no steam.

In winter, we unhitch the horses from the sleds they have been pulling and tie them up in the shed. In our cutter, Dad keeps a lined cowhide that is mostly black with some white. We use it as a lap robe when we're riding in the sleigh. When we get to the shed, we put the cowhide over the horse till we get back. Even though the blanket smells a little of horse, there sure is something awfully nice about having a little bit of warmth left on the blanket from the horse for our cutter trip home. Actually, the smell of horse isn't a bad smell. I kind of like it.

In wintertime, the one-mile, north-to-south dirt road next to our house sure gets some awfully high snowbanks. Sometimes, the snowplows pile up so much snow on both sides that, when another snowstorm piles even more snow between the snowbanks, the snowplows can't move any more snow on top of the already high snowbanks. There are two machines used to move snow—snowplows and snowblowers. Of course the snowplow just pushes snow.

There aren't very many snowblowers in the Ellenburgs. They sure are scary. One time a kid who wasn't seen by the driver of the snowblower was chopped up; at least that's what we heard in whispers. Maybe the whispers were to try and keep us out of the road. During the winter blizzards, the howling wind whips up sheets of bitterly cold snow as the roads are packed with ever-rising snow. When there is a very bad blizzard, I sure don't like it because then there isn't any school. Kids seem to fight more and parents seem to yell more when there is no school.

One of our neighbors, the Curry family, has a son who married a city slicker. We had heard about skiing but, of course, had never seen anyone do it, even though our farm is on the north side of the Adirondack Mountains and we have our own little mountain in the day pasture. The city woman brought skis with her from wherever she came from. With all the rocks and tree stumps, and her having to climb the mountain, she tried skiing down our little mountain only once.

I love our land so much. I love everything about it—the sights and the smells. I love the big and little rocks, the trees, the maple bush, the few spruce trees, the delicate little purple violets in the spring, and even the paintbrushes, which are considered weeds by most people. I love the fields of hay and how very pretty the first snow makes everything look, even though, in my heart, I know it won't be long before the harshness of winter sets in. Winter lasts for such a long time, but spring and summer will come.

32

Getting Mail ~ Ma's Pet

Sometimes I'm pretty sad and sometimes I cry. When I cry, I try not to let anybody see me. I wish there were somebody I could talk to. I think that maybe some of the other kids feel the same way. Rose always seems pretty happy. I wonder if it's because she always seems to make Ma happy. I still like Rose a lot, but it's hard not to be jealous. After all, being jealous is a sin. I try to make Ma like me, but it doesn't seem to work for me like it does for Rose. Maybe I should try a little harder, like doing less in the barn and helping more in the house. Of course, that would be really hard because I love all the animals, and Dad doesn't yell at me. Ma seems to get mad at me real easy.

The sink in the downstairs bathroom at our house is kind of scary. There is a medicine cabinet over the sink that has a mirror on it. On each side of the medicine cabinet is an electric fixture with a little metal arm that holds a light bulb. Of course, we kids have been told a lot of times not to climb up on the sink. But who wouldn't want to see what he or she looks like if a tooth has just fallen out? Something else we all were told is that, if we reach up and hang on to the light fixture, then use the other hand to hold onto a faucet, we could get an electric shock. I had a missing tooth and sure wanted to see what I looked like, so I took the chance anyway. I climbed up on the sink by holding onto one of the light fixtures. As I climbed down, I had one hand on the light fixture and the other hand touched a facet. When I got the shock, I jerked my hands away and fell into a clothes basket on the floor. It sure didn't feel good. That wasn't one of the things I ever did again—and I never told Ma about it, either.

Getting mail in our mailbox is so wonderful. If there is mail, the mailman puts it in the box and stands up the little metal flag on our mailbox. When we pick up the mail, we put the flag back down. If we have something for the mailman to pick up, we put it in the mailbox and put the flag up and he knows to stop even if he has no mail for us. After he does the pickup, he puts the flag down.

The mailman is the father of our teacher Miss Carpenter. They live in Ellenburg Center about a quarter mile down a short road that runs north off the main tar road that runs east and west. The main road passes through all three Ellenburgs, with the village farthest west being Ellenburg Center. About three and one-half miles east of Ellenburg Center is Ellenburg Corners, then about another mile and one-half east is Ellenburg Depot. The mailman uses a horse and sled in winter and a horse and buggy in summer. Every kid loves to get the mail, so that is one of the chores that gets done without anybody being told to do it. A lot of times, even though there isn't any mail in the box, kids check anyway two or three times in one day.

A most treasured letter to come in the mail is from one of my mother's sisters. They don't write to each other very often. My mother has four Benedictine nun sisters in St. Marys, Pennsylvania; a brother and a sister in Buffalo; a brother who's a sailor; a disabled brother who lives with my grandmother; a brother on a dairy farm; and one sister who died, leaving behind four children. We never get any mail from my mother's brothers or any of my father's relatives.

Catalogs are the very best of all the mail. If we are really lucky, the Sears Roebuck, the Montgomery Ward, and the Spiegel catalogs might come at sometime during the year. Of course, we aren't supposed to look at pages where almost bare bodies show bras, panties, and things like that. Catalogs, when they do come, seem to disappear quickly. I expect Sam has something to do with that.

Something that bothers me a lot is that Rose always seems to get whatever store-bought clothes might be ordered from a catalog. Rose is fifty-one weeks older than I, but that doesn't mean she should get every single new piece of clothes while I get hand-me-downs from older sisters. One time, there was a pair of peach-colored pajamas that came. I don't really know who they were for, but I sure knew that I wanted them really bad. I was pretty darn sure that they were meant for Rose. To make sure that she didn't get them, I managed to sneak them into a closet that opens into a hall at the head of the stairs on the kitchen side of the house.

The closet starts under a slanting roof. The area is about five and a half feet high to the far wall about eight feet away, which is about two and a half feet high. The hall stretches to the left into the darkness. I can't see where it ends. We keep things like kerosene lamps and ceramic jugs for pickling in that closet, but certainly not clothes. It was so dark in the closet that, when I went in, I stuffed the peach-colored pajamas into whatever was there. No one found them for years and, of course, who knew how they got there? I sure wasn't going to tell anybody.

On one side of the hall is the door into Ma and Dad's room, where they usually sleep together. Ma's feather bed is sometimes moved into the parlor—after she has another baby or when she is mad at Dad. The bed has a big, fat feather mattress. After somebody sleeps on it, the feathers get lumped up in the parts where the person didn't lie down. Whenever that bed is made up, it has to be shaken and poked to get the feathers fluffed up again.

On the south side of the hall at the head of the stairs is the bathroom door. In winter that bathroom isn't used very much for taking a bath. It isn't like the bathroom downstairs, which has its own little stove on a wooden table. With so many kids and Ma and Dad using the bathrooms, there sure is a lot of pounding on the doors when there are slowpokes inside. How long should it take for just a potty? Actually, sometimes if I need to sit for a little while, it is hard to get anything to read. Even a cleanser can to look at is better than nothing.

A very scary thing happened in the closet at the head of the back stairs. There is a brick chimney from the kitchen stove that goes through the floor of the closet and on up through the roof. In winter, when it is bitter cold with a howling north wind blowing, the kitchen stove is kept going full blast in an attempt to keep us warm. The chimney bricks get very hot. We all know about the awful things that happen if a brick chimney gets hot enough to start a fire. One time, that chimney was *that* hot. Boy, did Sam and Dad rush into the closet with buckets of water, wet blankets and towels. They managed to keep the house from burning down. I sure had a lot of bad dreams after that about our house burning down. But, then, I have some good dreams too, like the ones about galloping my horse Kit across a field, or being the first one to get to the mailbox and find a catalog in it.

Sometimes I dream in color. No painting that I have ever seen is so beautiful. It is as if the blue of the sky, the green of the trees and fields—everything—is touched with a kind of shimmering intense glow. The flowers are decorated with tints of sparkle mixed into their reds, blues, yellows, and purples. Why can I dream such pretty dreams, but I can't paint pictures the same way I dream? I do take such pains in school to use soft colors and paints when Miss Carpenter gives us pretty pictures to color. I don't think I'll ever be able to paint like my dreams, but I sure like the colors I can use from the crayons in my pencil box.

Maybe some day I'll have a house with a lot of pretty flowers around it.

33

Church ~ Heaven ~ Hell ~ Sins

What would it be like if I had beautiful teeth like my sister Rose instead of missing two teeth next to my two front teeth? How awful it sometimes makes me feel. I can't wait to grow up and get my teeth fixed in some way so that they will look like other people's teeth. I sure hope there is a way. I wonder why I have teeth like that. Nobody ever came right out and said that it might be because I had done something bad, but maybe that's what my mother thinks, because sometimes she says I am bad. Quite often in a sermon, the priest says God works in mysterious ways. I wonder if the way my teeth are has to do with God and maybe it's God's will. Nobody in my family, or in my school, or in the catechism classes at church has two missing teeth. I really think, in my heart, that I'm a very good girl. I can't think of anything really bad I've ever done.

Of course, in confession, to stay out of purgatory, I have to tell about fighting with my brothers and sisters. I don't think that would be bad enough to send me to hell. But, even *thinking* awfully bad thoughts might get me all the way to hell if I'm not careful. One time, Sam swung a bucket at me when I jumped out from in back of the washroom door to "boo" him. I was just playing. The bucket hit my arm so hard, I thought it might be broken. For a while, I wished he was dead. I sure had to tell that one in confession before I died or I might have ended up in hell forever. I know I shouldn't wonder about a lot of things because that could be a sin too. That's what the priest and Ma said, so I guess it must be true.

Does hell really hurt like when I hurt from burns here on earth, where even a little burn from a hot iron hurts so much? It must be awful in hell, where people burn all over their bodies or their souls. The church teaches us that our soul is what burns because when our body dies our soul leaves it and goes to one of three places: heaven or hell or purgatory. I'm not at all sure about souls being able to burn all over. What's a soul? What does it look like? How can it be happy or sad or hurt after people die? I'd better stop. After all, if I decide not to believe all that stuff, that might be enough for God to punish me and not even let me get into heaven no matter how good I've been in other ways. This whole thing can get pretty scary. I sure can't talk about any of this with anybody. If the priest says things on the altar about being damned to hell, then I guess it must be true.

It seems to me that, when big people want kids to do something, whether it's the priest, parents, or even brothers and sisters, every once in a while the "damned to hell" words came out one way or another. Of course, the priest, when he gives long sermons on Sunday, is the one who most often uses those words. Most of the time, I have good feelings in church, but sometimes I feel bad if the priest is talking a lot about sin, or is raising his voice really loud about people doing or not doing what he wants. Sometimes he hollers about people coming to church only on days like Christmas and Easter, and sometimes he hollers to make people give more money in the collection plate, or for a special drive for something like a new roof for the church.

In all of St. Edmund's parish there is not one other family that has twelve kids. Our pew is the fourth seat from the front on the left side of the aisle on the right side of the church. Of course, there are always too many kids, so we spill over to the seats in front and back and sometimes across the aisle. The row in back of ours has a big post near the aisle that we have to scrunch around in order to sit directly in back of our pew. Because all the rows have been assigned to certain people, when the Patnode bunch spills over into other people's pews and the people assigned to them show up for mass, they look pretty mad. If I happen be one of the kids who is sitting in somebody else's pew, and I have to move because someone looks at me funny, I feel particularly awful and embarrassed. I wonder if my brothers and sisters feel the same way.

There aren't very many people who go to church every single Sunday. Instead, some parishioners come only on very special days like Christmas when baby Jesus was born, and Easter Sunday when he came back to life—even though missing mass on Sunday is a sin unless there is a good reason, like being very sick. Another term the priest and my parents use is "fallen-away Catholics." I think that means that people have stopped going to church.

The fact that it's a sin to think bad thoughts sure makes it hard to stay in a state of grace. That is something we kids sure know about. We have to stay in a state of grace all the time in order to be able to be sure to get to heaven if we die from an accident. It's hard not to think bad thoughts. Sometimes I very much want to punch someone who is very mean, or sometimes I might want to try to flirt with a boy. Of course, there isn't anything I can possibly do that isn't going to be seen by some sister or brother and then tattled back to Ma and the other kids. I sure hear about anything that they think might be flirting. If I talk to Clarence or Ross, or any boy, everybody is sure I am flirting. I hate the terms "boy crazy" and "tomboy," especially when they are said in a very mean way. I wonder if kids like Antoinette ever hear words about sin or being boy crazy from her family. Sometimes wondering about things like that makes me jealous of some of the other kids.

The best thing about church is that I just know that God is there and that, even if other people like my mother don't seem to know what a very good girl I am, God knows. He and I talk. Well, actually it is me talking to him, but I know he hears and understands. While kneeling at the alter rail when the white little round flat bread that is God is placed on my tongue and it melts in my mouth, I know he is sure to hear everything I have to say to him. Actually, I think he hears me from the time I first get into the church, but my voice to God probably is much louder when I'm receiving Holy Communion.

Organ playing and singing in church is mostly done by one or more people in the Lashway family The aunt plays the piano and the Lashways, who live about a third of a mile north of our schoolhouse on the east side of the road, seem to have all the kids with the good voices. Monica is the best. She sings so nicely during mass. I never sing very loud unless it is with a bunch of kids because, if somebody like my brother Sam were to hear a part of a song where my voice goes up when it should go down, or the other way around, he would make fun of me forever. I'm not going to let that happen.

Being in a play in our schoolhouse is very different from singing in church where I might be made fun of. I love being in a play. When I get a part, it helps to make Christmas a happier time for me. It's a good thing that my brothers and sisters don't know how much I like having a part in a play, because I know they would call that being a show-off.

All I have to do is learn all the lines that I need to know for the play. The play isn't very long, and the most that any of us has to learn isn't very much, and Miss Carpenter is there following along. She whispers to kids to get them started on lines they forget.

I've never been to a movie, but I've heard about them. Maybe making movies would be something I'd like to do when I grow up. I could start over and be somebody else where nobody knows anything about me. I'm not sure what I want, except for people to just know me separate from my family. I think that probably people would like me.

Do other kids think about lots of different things? I wish I knew.

34

Mass ~ Good Catholic

I wonder why everybody who isn't a Catholic will go to hell. Protestants like Miss Carpenter and the man who owns the store with my Uncle Bill act as if they don't know about that. I don't think they believe that they are going to hell when they don't go to church every Sunday or when they commit sins like eating meat on Friday. I wonder what will happen to them when they die. They seem like nice people.

My mother and father are very interested in trying to convert anybody who isn't a Catholic. Mostly it is my mother who talks about that. After all, if somebody converts even one person to Catholicism, they are definitely going to go to heaven. I wonder if I could do a whole lot of sins after converting someone and never have to worry again about going to hell. What if the person you convert becomes a fallen-away Catholic? There are people who are supposed to be regular Catholics but who don't go to church very often. Do God and the church consider them fallen-away Catholics?

People who are good Catholics and who raise their kids with daily prayers, go to mass every Sunday, don't eat meat on Fridays, and go to confession sure should go to heaven. If their kids, when they grow up, go to church on only Christmas then take Communion without going to confession to tell about all their sins for the year, does that count against the mother and father? The kids must have an awful lot of sins collected over a whole year, so I think that might be pretty bad for the mother and father as well as the kids. It sure makes the priest mad when people show up at church only once or twice a year. I think the priest considers them fallen-away Catholics who are just making believe they are still good Catholics.

Every time there is a special mass on days like Christmas and Easter, the priest wears an extra fancy garment. First he puts on a cassock that looks like a long black dress that goes down to his ankles. Then he puts on a stiff white Roman collar that covers his throat. Next is a white, cotton, floor-length surplice tied at the waist; then a stole with a fringe on each end, which he puts around the back of his neck and crosses in front. The last garment is in the shape of a huge bib with a back and a front that goes over the priest's head and comes to just above his knees and is tied on each side. It has a silky sheen, and light reflects from its beautifully colored embroidery.

I do believe that men and boys are the ones who keep families together on almost every farm because I don't think that women and girls could ever keep a farm running by themselves with some of the heavy chores that have to be done. There are things like chopping wood, cutting down trees, shoeing horses, and plowing that not very many women and girls can do. It still doesn't seem right that we can never be altar girls or touch the priest's mass garments that are laid out in long, deep, flat drawers in the sacristy. It's not that I want to touch the garments; I just don't want to be told that I can't.

The reason I know about the drawers is that they are in the same room where there is a two-sided confessional. Sometimes the drawers are open when we're sitting waiting to go to confession. The room is on the east side of the main altar and in back of the Saint Joseph altar. On its east and west walls are chairs for people waiting to go into the confessional on the south wall. On the north wall are the silk-lined drawers that hold some of the robes the priest wears when he says mass. Over those drawers is a special miniature church-faced cupboard where the chalice holding the Eucharist is kept when it isn't in its little house on the main altar.

The room on the west side of the main altar and in back of the Virgin Mary's altar is where the altar boys change into long-sleeved, ankle-length red cassocks and loose, white, blousy tops that go down to their elbows and a little below their waist. These boys serve as altar boys at mass. I sure would love to be an altar girl. My oldest brother Sam and my younger brother Joe always seem so proud to be up there on the altar. They have special things to do during the mass besides kneel on the steps facing the altar. They get to do things like pour water and wine into the chalice at certain times during the mass.

There are other things in the closets that hold the priest and altar boys' clothes on the north wall in the room west of the main altar. In part of one closet are shelves that hold things like candles. People buy candles as offerings to God. They light them in front of a statue at home during prayers. In the main part of the church in the front of the Mother Mary and Saint Joseph side alters there are candle holders where people pay to light candles usually as an offering for a special intention such as for a sick person to get well. Now back to the room on the west side of the main alter. There are bottles of holy water, vases for flowers, kids'

First Holy Communion prayer books, novena cards, and statues that people can buy to take home. People keep the statues on top of furniture like our buffet and often say daily prayers kneeling in front them. There are statues of God holding his heart, the Virgin Mary holding out her arms with the palms of her hands in an upright position, Saint Joseph holding a staff, and Saint Christopher. We pray to Saint Christopher to help us find things, and to other saints, like Saint Theresa, for special intentions.

Inside a glass-covered case in the middle of the floor are other things that people can buy like rosaries, medals, and scapulars for people to wear. Of course, my mother and father, whenever they buy anything, make sure to get it blessed by the priest in order to get blessings for the person wearing or using the article. Scapulars are two little two-by-two-and-one-half-inch pieces of brown cloth with holy pictures printed on them. There are two very thin brown ribbons about one and one-half feet long running from each side of the little cloth to the other little cloth. The two thin ribbons go on each side of a person's neck, with one little cloth in front and one little cloth in back. Any kid in my family who is going to wear a scapular wears a metal scapular medal that is supposed to give the same blessing as a cloth one. My mother and grandmother both wear the cloth scapular rather than a medal one because they think there is more of a blessing that comes from a cloth scapular. I don't know why and I sure can't ask either of them.

In addition to a scapular, my mother wears a very special medal that Little Rose Ferron gave her when my mother and father visited her home. Miss Ferron is a mystic who lives in Woonsocket, Rhode Island. At certain times of the year, such as just before Easter, she bleeds from the same places that Jesus did when he was dying on the cross. She seems to be bleeding as if she has the crown of thorns on her head and nails in her hands and feet. My mother and father have a great devotion to Little Rose. Our pastor in Saint Edmund Church, Father Boyer, wrote a book about her, *She Wears a Crown of Thorns*, and is gathering information in order to try and have her declared a saint at some time in the future. Any story about a person who has prayed for a special cause and looked for heavenly intervention through her and thinks that something miraculous has occurred, encourages a lot of people to believe that, in future years, she might be declared a saint. My mother wears the medal from Little Rose on a chain. The outside is about a half inch across and is in the shape of a rose. It slides open to show the same saints that are on a scapular as well as what is on a miraculous medal. My mother wears the medal all the time—even when she is taking a bath.

Something that is quite wonderful about the room on the west side of the main altar is that the room usually has the faint smell of beeswax candles and incense. One of the best smells in the world is when, at a church service, the priest lights incense in a special metal pot that hangs from a chain, then walks down the church aisle moving the pot from side to side as incense smoke comes out of the little holes in the top of the pot.

Girls don't very often see the room on the left of the altar where the boys change clothes and there are religious things to buy. After all, our family isn't going to be buying something like a prayer book for our First Holy Communion more than once for each of us, and people aren't going to keep buying new statues. Our First Holy Communion is very special. We each get our very own little catechism prayer book and a framed picture, about eighteen inches by ten inches, of Jesus holding his heart outside of his body in front of his chest. Our name is written under Jesus' picture. We will have been getting ready for a long time. There are catechism lessons in which we learn more about Jesus, Mary, and Joseph. Other things we need to know are the Ten Commandments and what we have to do to stay in a state of grace. Actually, we hear enough about bad things from Ma to already know that part. It's very important to not have any sins on our souls when we receive our First Holy Communion. Of course, we all need to be in a state of grace when we receive Holy Communion.

The catechism classes sometimes are actually kind of fun. We can get water to drink in back of the rectory next to the church, where there is a big four-and-one-half-foot-high iron pump with a tin cup hanging from it. There is a two-foot-long handle at the side of the pump.

There is a three-inch spout in the middle of the pump where the water comes out. It is fun to pump the handle with water splashing into the cup as well as down onto the cement base. Of course, if no grownup is around, the little kids are likely to get soaked from the big kids splashing water on them. Big kids seem to like to make little kids cry, which is fun for the big kids and not much fun for the little kids. I'm pretty darn sure the big kids never admit it as a sin by telling the priest in confession.

Sometimes it's fun being a kid and sometimes it's no fun at all.

35

Wishes ~ Baby Animals

I want a horse so badly. I know that, out of my whole family, I'm the one who likes animals the best. In fact, I don't think there is another kid who really loves animals enough to want a cat to sleep on his or her bed. Well, I guess I really don't know for sure about that one. After all, Ma never lets dogs in the house, and she lets cats in only once in a while to catch mice. When cats are allowed in the house, Ma makes sure they are kept in the cellar, which has a cold, earthen floor. Mostly, cats are outdoors or in the barn. Sam thinks it's pretty darn funny when he is milking a cow and he squirts milk in the direction of a cat many feet away and the cat just sits there trying to lap the milk which has been squirted all over its head. Some of the cats just run away when the milk hits them. Sam thinks that is funny too. Of course, he never puts milk in a pan for them.

In particular, what I want is a baby horse—a little colt. It would come out of a mare—like in the veterinary book where a baby horse is half out of its mother. Once in a while, when nobody is around, I sneak a look at that book, wishing the picture was of one of our girl horses, Queen or Kit, having a baby.

The book is on the wooden mantle of the redbrick fireplace in the parlor right next to a two-foot St. Theresa statue. The statue stands in a beautiful wooden frame that my dad built. It is open in the front and has a solid one-and-one-half-inch-wide maple wood edging that rises from the base and curves over her head. The same edging frames the back. Holding the two solid wood framing pieces together are small wooden slats about one-half inch wide and six inches long. Mostly, we say our family prayers—with all the kneeling—in front of the Sacred Heart of Jesus statue on the buffet in the dining room rather than in front of the St. Theresa statue.

We aren't supposed to see things like a calf coming out of its mother when it is happening in the barn, and we aren't supposed to look at the big veterinary book. I think that somehow it's supposed to be dirty or something. I wonder if any of the other kids ever look at that big fat book when there isn't anybody else around.

I'll bet Rose never does, and I suspect that most of my other brothers and sisters aren't curious enough to want to.

I just love baby animals so much. One time, a pair of twin calves was born on our farm. They weren't real small, but I was pretty sure that they weren't big enough for my father to keep because they probably wouldn't grow up to be good milking cows. I sure coaxed. They were a lot more black than white, while most calves are born with a lot more white than black. They were so beautiful. Dad just kind of mumbled and, of course, a couple of days later when I went to the barn they were gone.

The calves that are almost always sent out to be killed for meat are the boy calves. After all, most farms have just one bull and sometimes one boy calf. When they are first born, calves are all so darling, with their shiny little noses and stuck-up little ears. When I put my hand in front of them, they suck on my fingers. For a couple of days after a calf is born, we put their mother's milk in a bucket to give to the newborn calf because that milk can't be put in with the rest of the cows' milk to be sent to the milk plant. I'm not sure why.

When Dad is teaching a newborn calf to drink out of a bucket, he pushes its nose down into the milk in the bucket with one hand and puts his other hand into the milk and lets them suck it off his fingers. At first they jerk their heads up as bubbles rise from the milk. It takes a couple of days for calves to get the idea of how to drink.

I almost hate long winters. There sure is more than one reason. The cows aren't let out of their stanchions for all of the long, cold winter months. They aren't sprayed in the fall, so, by the middle of winter, they have big bumps on their backs from some kind of bug eggs that grow to big fat white grubs. The bumps have a quarter inch opening where sometimes I can see a tiny bit of the grub. In summer they dry up and disappear. The howling bitterly cold wind always seems to be fighting to get through any cracks it can find in both the house and the barn. There isn't anything I can do about letting the cows out of the barn in winter. Even though I am a big girl for my age, I am still just a big kid.

I so much want to do something different for all the animals on the farm in addition to turning them loose in the winter—like giving them fresh straw as soon as the backs of their stalls are dirty, having a heated place for the chickens instead of the icy chicken house part of the barn, untying the dog whose link chain keeps winding into a shorter and shorter length, choosing not to kill the pigs who keep one side of their pen clean as they potty on the other side, never hitting or kicking a horse or a cow or a dog or a cat. I wonder if anybody else ever thinks about things like that.

I sure ask God to do a lot of stuff, but nothing ever seems to change. I pray for a lot of other things besides things that have to do with the farm. There is always hell to worry about. The word "sin" seems to be everywhere in what the priest says during his sermons and in what Ma says.

I think maybe I'm close to God when I'm in the woods, whether I'm on horseback getting the cows or on foot picking berries. Every part of the forest has some really nice things about it, like the mysterious forest with its pretty, very-close-together little maple trees. There is the night pasture that is so rocky that only a few low blueberry bushes grow there. I could go on and on, but I've already told you a lot about the different parts of the farm and what they mean to me.

Back to the one thing that I want more than anything in the whole world—my very own little baby horse. I could give so much love to a little baby horse. Baby dogs, cats, cows, pigs, and chickens are all pretty wonderful, but a baby horse I would just love to bits. There never seems to be enough time to do a lot of stuff, but I just know that, if I had a baby horse, no matter what, somehow I would find time to give it a lot of attention with Ma using whatever extra time we have to pray—even in the car.

The one thing I don't dare ask my mother or father—or anyone else for that matter—is why, when we have both boy and girls horses, the girls never get pregnant. After all, sometimes all the horses are turned loose in the pasture together. My gray darling Kit is a girl. We have the one boy bull and the cows get pregnant. If only Kit would get pregnant. For a very long time, I'm sure I wouldn't have to be pushed to kneel up straight for prayers, and I sure would never eat on Sunday morning so I would be able to go to Communion at mass in thanksgiving to God. I'm sure it would be easier to not have bad thoughts, like the time I wished for Sam to die because he was so mean to me. Boy, that was sure a big one for confession. I wonder if other people have had sins that big to tell in confession.

36

Making Ice Cream

Farmers are paid by how much cream is in the milk they sell to Sealtest, as well as the amount of milk. The night milking is put into milk cans that are put in the water-filled cement tubs in the milk house for cooling overnight. By morning, the cream portion has settled at the top of the can. My father gets worried about taking cream off the top of the milk cans in the morning to make ice cream. It sure takes a lot of coaxing. We don't have a refrigerator, so it has to be at the right time of the year when there is still enough ice and snow to use in making the ice cream and when it's not so cold that we can't be outside on the porch cranking the handle on the top of the wooden bucket ice cream maker.

The handle is attached to a metal cylinder about eighteen inches long and eight inches across. A double, one-inch-wide wooden paddle edged in metal runs from the top to the bottom of the cylinder. We turn the paddle by the crank on top. The space between the cylinder and the wooden bucket is kept filled with ice and snow and sprinkles of salt. The salt keeps the ice and snow melting.

First, Ma cooks the ice cream mixture on the stove. It is pretty much like regular vanilla pudding except cream is used instead of milk. After we've poured it into the ice cream maker and begun to turn the crank, Ma has a hard time keeping us from opening the top every few minutes to see if it getting thick enough to start eating like regular ice cream. Crank, crank, crank the handle. We get so excited. After all, this doesn't happen more than once or twice a year. At last, the cover is lifted out with some of the ice cream stuck to the paddle. We all have spoons ready. Of course, there is still more waiting for the rest of the ice cream because Ma puts the cover back on and we have to wait for it to harden a little more. After the cranking, Ma sure has to be the one to give us our shares because I don't think any of us would try to get higher in heaven by getting less ice cream.

37

God and the Devil

Boys are allowed to be altar boys, but not us girls. I don't know why. I would be so proud if I could be serving as an alter girl during mass. I'm pretty sure that I would be called a show-off by somebody in my family, but I wouldn't care. My brother Sam is often an alter boy. There he is, up on the altar in a long red cassock with a shorter, white garment over the top. I'll bet the people in church never guess how mean he can be. When I think about things like that, I guess I should really be thinking about how he is already doing as much hard work on our farm as a hired man does. Some of the many chores he helps with are milking the cows, haying, and loading and spreading manure.

There are just so very many things that have to be done on a farm. As our family keeps getting bigger, we keep getting poorer. After a while we couldn't afford a hired man, and, when Sam was still a kid, he took over what had been done by the hired man. That's something I try to keep in mind, and I try not to stay awfully mad at Sam when he has been especially mean to me. In winter, hay has to be fed to all the animals in the morning, then again at night. In the spring, there is planting in addition to all the regular chores. During the summer, there is all the extra work of cutting then bringing the dried hay into the barn, threshing the stalks of the oat grain, and all kinds of things like that.

Even though Sam works pretty darn hard, all us older kids hear Ma and Dad sometimes whisper about some bad thing or other that Sam has done. I never hear exactly what they are saying, but I hear enough words to know they are pretty mad. But I never hear them say anything to Sam. Any time I want to know about something, I try to find out by asking my oldest sister, Rita, or any other older sister. The answer is usually the same—"You'll find out in your later years." I sure don't like to hear those words.

One thing about God that sure is a puzzle to me is that we are told about all his goodness and love for us, so how can bad things happen? It is probably the same question that even grown-ups have. How can things like people getting hurt in accidents or houses or barns burning down—all kinds of bad things that happen—if God can make everything be all right?

Sometimes bad things happen to me. I have fallen off a horse and gotten hurt. Sometimes people say awfully mean things, like I am possessed by the devil, when I know I'm a good girl. Why does God let people say things like that? What happens if somebody is really possessed by the devil? What an awful thought.

Something else we're told is that the devil is everywhere. If God is everywhere, how can the devil be everywhere? Why is God, who is called all powerful, let the devil be everywhere tempting everybody to be bad? I wonder if my mother and father are afraid of the devil—or are they afraid of God? I wonder if they ever think they have done anything bad. After all, they are the bosses of all us kids.

Grown-ups can do all kinds of things that kids can't. I just know that, when I'm a grownup, I can get people to like me. It's so hard to try and be liked with so many kids in my family and things like Ma liking Rose so much and nobody ever saying I love you or hugging or kissing. I'll bet city kids hear things like that. It seems to me that almost all farm families are so busy all the time that I don't think there is much said to each other. Of course, I don't have any way of knowing how different things might be for kids who don't live on a farm. I never hear about any of them having to do things like chores before they go to school.

When the farm boys—and sometimes girls—help with farm chores before school, their clothes almost certainly have at least a little bit of a barn smell. It's hard to be in a barn where the animals are pottying without the barn smell sticking to clothes. Whenever city kids visit a farm—kids like my Buffalo cousins—they always seem to be at least a little bit stuck up. They complain about smells or the dust from the hay, or that it's too cold or too hot. Everybody—my grandmother, my aunts in the convent, even my mother—brags about our Buffalo cousins as if they are better than us. When I grow up, I'll just have to be somebody special.

I sure wish that we didn't hear so often about how the devil is around us all the time using all kinds of temptations to try to get us to do all kinds of bad things. The devil is big on temptations, trying to get us to lie or steal or fight with our brothers or sisters. He has all kinds of ways to get us to sin. Why isn't God just as pushy trying to make us be good? Maybe he is and that's why the kids who don't do a lot of bad things are helped by God not to do bad things. The whole thing sure gets mixed up! Maybe I need to talk more often to my guardian angel.

Below is a dedication to Theresa M. Santmann (formerly known as Theresa Patnode) in MARYJANE'S IDEABOOK • COOKBOOK • LIFEBOOK.

Terry

If there are angels among us, Terry Santmann is mine. Sometimes referred to as an angel investor, Terry has been more than a financial hand-up to me. George Eliot said, "One must be poor to know the luxury of giving." Terry spent the first seventeen years of her life on a dairy farm, where her family of fourteen barely eked out a living. Winters were bitterly cold, and their poverty so searing, it stole all hope of betterment. So with eighteen dollars in her pocket, Terry left home, working every make-do job imaginable, from seamstress to taxicab driver. She eventually married, and three months into her second pregnancy, her husband was diagnosed with Lou Gehrig's disease. For many years, Terry cared for her quadriplegic husband and growing children by working part-time jobs. Even with her huge burden, Terry found time to spearhead a food drive for unemployed coal miners. "You can always find someone who needs help even more than you," she says. (Her list of community projects is long.) With twenty thousand dollars from insurance that paid out on doctors' assurances that her husband was terminally ill, Terry started an adult home with him as her first patient, doing everything from plumbing to bookkeeping. Eventually, she built new and larger nursing homes, always finding time to help others.

Terry, this is for you, for showing me that insurmountable isn't an option, that laughter and dancing are. (Don't think I didn't notice that at age seventy-one, you outdanced me at Meg's wedding.)

978-0-595-45747-2
0-595-45747-9